CRITICAL ANTHOLOGIES OF NONFICTION WRITING ™

CRITICAL PERSPECTIVES ON GLOBALIZATION

Edited by
Ann Malaspina

THE ROSEN PUBLISHING GROUP, INC.
NEW YORK

For the next generation, Sam, Nicholas, Alex, Lily, and Sofia.

Published in 2006 by The Rosen Publishing Group, Inc.
29 East 21st Street, New York, NY 10010

Copyright © 2006 by The Rosen Publishing Group, Inc.

First Edition

Library of Congress Cataloging-in-Publication Data

Critical perspectives on globalization/edited by Ann Malaspina.
    p. cm.—(Critical anthologies of nonfiction writing)
Includes bibliographical references and index.
ISBN 1-4042-0537-3 (library binding)
1. Globalization. 2. International economic integration.
I. Malaspina, Ann, 1957– II. Series.
JZ1318.C753 2006
337—dc22

                                                2005014706

Manufactured in the United States of America

On the cover: Don Hammond photographed this image in the 1990s.

CONTENTS

INTRODUCTION

I n the winter of 2005, a snowshoe factory in Vermont shut down operations. The employees were matter-of-fact about the news. They knew it was coming. Tubbs Snowshoes in Stowe, Vermont, had been in business since 1906, but despite a great reputation and successful new innovations in snowshoe design, the business could not compete with companies already manufacturing in China. The owner sold the business to K2, the sporting goods conglomerate, which operates a manufacturing complex in Guangzhou, China. Wages and operating costs are much lower in China than in Vermont, so the snowshoes would now be made in Guangzhou.

A Vermont factory moving to China is just one aspect of globalization, or the growing integration of economy, technology, and culture around the globe. From the Wal-Mart supercenter in Pohang City, South Korea, to the black Chilean grapes we can buy at a New Jersey supermarket, the signs of globalization are everywhere. We let the world into our living rooms and offices every minute, when we rely upon technology such as the Internet, twenty-four-hour cable news, and cell phones. What happens in one part of the world—whether it's a tsunami in Southeast Asia or crude oil production in the Middle East—affects people around the globe. As Scottish sociologist Roland Robertson writes in *Globalization: Social Theory and Global Culture*, globalization is "the compression of the world and the intensification of consciousness of the world as a whole."

With so much upheaval, globalization has ignited fierce debates. Antiglobalization protesters criticize the way that newly opened borders of trade and commerce have affected human rights, labor rights, poverty, inequality, and the environment. "Whenever I hear the phrase 'free trade,' I can't help picturing factories I visited in the Philippines and Indonesia that are all surrounded by gates, watchtowers, and soldiers—to keep the highly subsidized products from leaking out and the union organizers from getting in," writes Naomi Klein in "Don't Fence Us In." Others say that a globalized economy—and interconnected world—is the only way forward, and that most people will benefit in the long run. Closer contact between people around the world will lead to better understanding and the creation of a truly global village, they say. "Mexicans have the opportunity to drink Frappuccinos and contemplate pop art, while Americans can enjoy burritos and read the novels of Carlos Fuentes," writes Tyler Cowen, professor of economics at George Mason University, in "The Fate of Culture."

In fact, globalization is nothing new. As soon as people could travel beyond their hometowns, they sought new markets for their goods, often in faraway places. In exchange, they hoped to secure goods that they could not make or acquire at home. From the second century BC to the sixteenth century AD, traders traveled the 5,000-mile Silk Road, a set of trade routes leading from China to the Mediterranean Sea. Chinese traders brought precious silk, which the Europeans could not yet weave themselves, as well as gunpowder and paper. European traders carried gold to China in return. Yet goods were not the only items traded. Ideas were exchanged, too, as was religion. As trade increased, so did the integration of culture and customs, just like what's happening today.

The modern era of globalization took off after World War II. The World Bank and International Monetary Fund were created in 1944 and 1945, respectively, to help stabilize the world economy and encourage investment in countries with struggling economies. These global institutions lend money to developing countries for projects such as building roads, fighting disease, and providing clean water. In 1948, the General Agreement on Trade and Tariffs (GATT), later the World Trade Organization, began liberalizing trade rules and dropping tariffs, or taxes placed on imported goods to protect domestic industries.

The fall of the Berlin Wall in 1989 increased the pace of globalization. With the end of the Cold War and Communism in Eastern Europe, more countries were able to join the world marketplace. In Russia, for example, state industries were taken over by private owners eager to test the waters of capitalism. Interdependence between nations quickened with establishment of the European Union in 1992 and the North American Free Trade Agreement (NAFTA) in 1994. NAFTA created a free-trade zone in the United States, Canada, and Mexico, gradually eliminating tariffs on goods and services produced in North America. Critics of NAFTA feared that the United States would lose jobs to Mexico, and that Mexico would experience environmental problems as more industry developed there. More than a decade later, NAFTA remains controversial. Meanwhile, China broke from its historic policies of isolationism to encourage private companies to build factories and export goods. Powered by a huge workforce, China's economy grew rapidly. In 2001, the Communist nation joined the World Trade Organization.

Globalization is also an information revolution allowing anyone with a computer access to data and products from around the world. The Internet and the World Wide Web opened the flow of information starting in the 1990s, allowing ordinary citizens to access a global market that seems to have no limits. News, financial information, culture, ideas, and goods became available to anyone with a computer and an e-mail address. The number of Web sites grew from 500 in 1994 to nearly 3 billion in 2000, according to Microsoft chairman Bill Gates. "The Internet has already revolutionized the way we live and work, but it is still in its infancy," predicted Gates in "Shaping the Internet Age."

The pace of globalization is so fast today that it is difficult to comprehend, much less control. Yet those watching its progress have raised many serious questions. Yale University law professor Amy Chua warns that exporting American wealth, values, and democracy to developing countries can sometimes ignite resentment and even violence. ". . . Anti-Americanism is often a perverse blend of admiration, awe, and envy on one hand and seething hatred, disgust, and contempt on the other," she writes in *World on Fire: How Exporting Free Market Democracy Breeds Ethnic Hatred and Global Instability*. Chua urges that more attention must be paid to the volatility of unequal power and wealth in a democratizing world.

Many people worry that the world's poor have been left behind in a globalized economy. In 2004, the United Nations released a report stating that international trade has not reduced poverty in the least developed nations, and that increased exports have not benefited the poor in those countries. The World Bank, with its mission to rescue the poor nations of the world, has often been the target of bitter attacks. Critics say it has failed in its mandate, instead using its power and financial resources to enrich wealthy nations and multinational corporations. "The major financial institutions of globalization have failed to save the struggling countries they were . . . meant to serve," writes economist Joseph E. Stiglitz in *Globalization and Its Discontents*. Stiglitz won the Nobel Prize in Economics in 2001.

Determined to do better, the former World Bank president James D. Wolfensohn acknowledges that more must be done to empower the poor in developing countries. "We cannot turn back globalization; our challenge is to make it an instrument of opportunity and inclusion, not of fear and insecurity," he writes in his essay, "A Call to Global Action." To combat the uncertainties spawned by globalization, such as sudden job losses in the United States and an increase in inequality in developing countries, *New York Times* foreign affairs columnist Thomas L. Friedman cautions that care must be taken. In *The Lexus and the Olive Tree: Understanding Globalization*, he urges a "sustainable globalization" that provides safety nets to those at risk of being left behind.

Protecting the environment has become a huge challenge. Clean water supplies, biodiversity, and rain forests are all impacted by new development and trade. Newly opened markets often spark more exports of wood, minerals, and other natural resources, leading to deforestation, water pollution, and other degradation. Also, increased industry in developing countries without environmental laws poses risks to the air, water, and earth, critics say. Nongovernmental organizations, such as Friends of the Earth, are pushing for sustainable development that does not harm the environment. In South Africa, the group is helping local residents monitor air quality around oil refineries and push for safer air quality standards. The World Bank is also trying to combine economic development with environmental protection. For example, the World Bank and the Brazilian government are working on a project to conserve the Brazilian rain forest. This project is seeking to reduce logging and protect the land of native peoples while still promoting economic growth.

As the twenty-first century unfolds, the forces of globalization will keep pushing forward, creating a world that is more complex and intertwined. The call now is to make globalization improve the lives of as many people as possible. As we've already seen, a more connected world opens the door for positive change. In many developing countries, infant mortality rates have fallen, life expectancy has risen, and fewer people are illiterate, according to a 2001 report by the International Monetary Fund. International programs to fight AIDS, vaccinate children, improve literacy, ban child labor, and protect endangered species have made great progress, but most people agree that more has to be done. As former U.S. president Jimmy Carter said in his Nobel Peace Prize acceptance speech in 2002, "The bond of our common humanity is stronger than the divisiveness of our fears and prejudices." —*AM*

CHAPTER ONE

POWER, AUTHORITY, AND GOVERNANCE: THE ROLE OF GOVERNMENTS AND CORPORATIONS IN GLOBALIZING THE WORLD

Globalization was a new concept when British sociologist Anthony Giddens began writing about it in the 1980s. Giddens, director of the London School of Economics from 1997 to 2003, sees globalization as a natural, mostly positive consequence of the modern age, driven by advances in communication and information technologies. With its progress, he argues, women have gained new freedoms; democracy has taken hold in more countries; and wealth has spread, at least for some. Globalization has also made the world smaller, with faraway events influencing local economies and politics. Yet, as people are forced into contact with others who may not share their values, clashes can occur. Globalization is "the intensification of world-wide social relationships," Giddens writes in Runaway World: How Globalization Is Reshaping Our Lives. *People are struggling to adjust to the dramatic changes that have occurred at home, in the workplace, in their nations, and in the world. "We are living through a major period of historical transition," writes Giddens. —AM*

From *Runaway World: How Globalization Is Reshaping Our Lives*
by Anthony Giddens
2000

A friend of mine studies village life in central Africa. A few years ago, she paid her first visit to a remote area where she was to carry out her fieldwork. The day she arrived, she was invited to a local home for an evening's entertainment. She expected to find out about the traditional pastimes of this isolated community. Instead, the occasion turned out to be a viewing of *Basic Instinct* on video. The film at that point hadn't even reached the cinemas in London.

Such vignettes reveal something about our world. And what they reveal isn't trivial. It isn't just a matter of people adding modern paraphernalia—videos, television sets, personal computers and so forth—to their existing ways of life. We live in a world of transformations, affecting almost every aspect of what we do. For better or worse, we are being propelled into a global order that no one fully understands, but which is making its effects felt upon all of us.

Globalization may not be a particularly attractive or elegant word. But absolutely no one who wants to understand our prospects at century's end can ignore it. I travel a lot to speak abroad. I haven't been to a single country recently where globalization isn't being intensively discussed. In France, the word is *mondialisation*. In Spain and Latin America, it is *globalzación*. The Germans say *Globalisierung*.

The global spread of the term is evidence of the very developments to which it refers. Every business guru talks about it. No political speech is complete without reference to it. Yet even in the late 1980s the term was hardly used, either in the academic literature or in everyday language. It has come from nowhere to be almost everywhere.

Given its sudden popularity, we shouldn't be surprised that the meaning of the notion isn't always clear, or that an intellectual reaction has set in against it. Globalization has something to do with the thesis that we now all live in one world—but in what way exactly, and is the idea really valid? Different thinkers have taken almost completely opposite views about globalization in debates that have sprung up over the past few years. Some dispute the whole thing. I'll call them the skeptics.

According to the skeptics, all the talk about globalization is only that—just talk. Whatever its benefits, its trials and tribulations, the global economy isn't especially different from that which existed at previous periods. The world carries on much the same as it has done for many years.

Most countries, the skeptics argue, gain only a small amount of their income from external trade. Moreover, a good deal of economic exchange is between regions, rather than being truly world-wide. The countries of the European Union, for example, mostly trade among themselves. The same is true of the other main trading blocs, such as those of Asia-Pacific or North America.

Others take a very different position. I'll label them the radicals. The radicals argue that not only is globalization very real, but that its consequences can be felt everywhere. The global market-place, they say, is much more developed than in the 1960s and 1970s and is indifferent to national borders. Nations have lost most of the sovereignty they once had, and politicians have lost most of their capability to influence events. It isn't surprising that no one respects political leaders any more, or has much interest in what they have to say. The era of the nation-state is over. Nations, as the Japanese business writer Kenichi Ohmae puts it, have become mere "fictions." Authors such as Ohmae see the economic difficulties of the 1998 Asian crisis as demonstrating the reality of globalization, albeit seen from its disruptive side.

The skeptics tend to be on the political left, especially the old left. For if all of this is essentially a myth, governments can still control economic life and the welfare state remain intact. The notion of globalization, according to the skeptics, is an ideology put about by free-marketers who wish to dismantle welfare systems and cut back on state expenditures. What has happened is at most a reversion to how the world was a century ago. In the late nineteenth century there was already an open global economy, with a great deal of trade, including trade in currencies.

Well, who is right in this debate? I think it is the radicals. The level of world trade today is much higher than it ever was before, and involves a much wider range of goods and services. But the biggest difference is in the level of finance and capital flows. Geared as it is to electric money—money that exists only as digits in computers—the current world economy has no parallels in earlier times.

In the new global electronic economy, fund managers, banks, corporations, as well as millions of individual investors, can transfer vast amounts of capital from one side of the world to another at the click of a mouse. As they do so, they can destabilize what might have seemed rock-solid economies—as happened in the events in Asia.

The volume of world financial transactions is usually measured in US dollars. A million dollars is a lot of money for most people. Measured as a stack of hundred dollar notes, it would be eight inches high. A billion dollars—in other words, a thousand million—would stand higher than St. Paul's Cathedral. A trillion dollars—a million million—would be over 120 miles high, 20 times higher than Mount Everest.

Yet far more than a trillion dollars is now turned over *each day* on global currency markets. This is a massive increase from only the late 1980s, let alone the more distant past. The value of whatever money we may have in our pockets, or our bank accounts, shifts from moment to moment according to fluctuations in such markets.

I would have no hesitation, therefore, in saying that globalization, as we are experiencing it, is in many respects not only new, but also revolutionary. Yet I don't believe that either the skeptics or the radicals have properly understood either what it is or its implications for us. Both groups see the phenomenon almost solely in economic terms. This is a mistake. Globalization is political, technological, and cultural, as well as economic. It has been influenced above all by developments in systems of communication, dating back only to the late 1960s.

In the mid-nineteenth century, a Massachusetts portrait painter, Samuel Morse, transmitted the first message, "What hath God wrought?" by electric telegraph. In so doing, he initiated a new phase in world history. Never before could a message be sent without someone going somewhere to carry it. Yet the advent of satellite communications marks every bit as dramatic a break with the past. The first commercial satellite was launched only in 1969. Now there are more than 200 such satellites above the earth, each carrying a vast range of information. For the first time ever, instantaneous communication is possible from one side of the world to the other. Other types of electronic communication, more and more integrated with satellite transmission, have also accelerated over the past few years. No dedicated transatlantic or transpacific cables existed at all until the late 1950s. The first held fewer than 100 voice paths. Those of today carry more than a million.

On February 1, 1999, about 150 years after Morse invented his system of dots and dashes, Morse Code finally disappeared from the world stage. It was discontinued as a means of communication for the sea. In its place has come a system using satellite technology, whereby any ship in distress can be pinpointed immediately. Most countries prepared for the transition some while before. The French, for example, stopped using Morse Code in their local waters in 1997, signing off with a Gallic flourish: "Calling all. This is our last cry before our eternal silence."

Instantaneous electronic communication isn't just a way in which news or information is conveyed more quickly. Its existence alters the very texture of our lives, rich and poor alike. When the image of Nelson Mandela may be more familiar to us than the face of our next-door neighbor, something has changed in the nature of our everyday experience.

Nelson Mandela is a global celebrity, and celebrity itself is largely a product of new communications technology. The reach of media technologies is growing with each new wave of innovation. It took 40 years for radio in the United States to gain an audience of 50 million. The same number was using personal computers only 15 years after the personal computer was introduced. It needed a mere 4 years, after it was made available, for 50 million people to be regularly using the Internet.

It is wrong to think of globalization as just concerning the big systems, like the world financial order. Globalization isn't only about what is "out there," remote and far away from the individual. It is an "in here" phenomenon too, influencing intimate and personal aspects of our lives. The debate about family values, for example, that is going on in many countries might seem far removed from globalizing influences. It isn't. Traditional family systems are becoming transformed, or are under strain, in many parts of the world, particularly as women stake claim to greater equality. There has never before been a society, so far as we know from the historical record, in which women have been even approximately equal to men. This is a truly global revolution in everyday life, whose consequences are being felt around the world in spheres from work to politics.

Globalization thus is a complex set of processes, not a single one. And these operate in a contradictory or oppositional fashion. Most people think of globalization as simply "pulling away" power or influence from local communities and nations into the global arena. And indeed this is one of its consequences. Nations do lose some of the economic power they once had. Yet it also has an opposite effect. Globalization not only pulls upwards, but also pushes downwards, creating new pressures for local autonomy. The American sociologist Daniel Bell describes this very well when he says that the nation becomes not only too small to solve the big problems, but also too large to solve the small ones.

Globalization is the reason for the revival of local cultural identities in different parts of the world. If one asks, for example, why the Scots want more independence in the UK, or why there is a strong separatist movement in Quebec, the answer is not to be found only in their cultural history. Local nationalisms spring up as a response to globalizing tendencies, as the hold of older nation-states weakens.

Globalization also squeezes sideways. It creates new economic and cultural zones within and across nations. Examples are the Hong Kong region, northern Italy, and Silicon Valley in California. Or consider the Barcelona region. The area around Barcelona in northern Spain extends into France. Catalonia, where Barcelona is located, is closely integrated into the European Union. It is part of Spain, yet it also looks outwards.

These changes are being propelled by a range of factors, some structural, others more specific and historical. Economic influences are certainly among the driving forces—especially the global financial system. Yet they aren't like forces of nature. They have been shaped by technology, and cultural diffusion, as well as by the decisions of governments to liberalize and deregulate their national economies.

———■———

The North American Free Trade Agreement (NAFTA) is a regional agreement between Canada, Mexico, and the United States to implement a free-trade area. Designed to eliminate trade and investment barriers, NAFTA is also intended to promote fair competition, increase investment opportunities, and establish cooperation between the three countries. Long before it went into effect on January 1, 1994, NAFTA was intensely controversial. Supporters said it would provide new trade and investment opportunities, while critics predicted it would lead to the loss of U.S. jobs, privatization of public utilities like water, and gains for the rich but not the poor in Mexico, not to mention an increase in the U.S. trade deficit. More than a decade later, NAFTA is still polarizing. Still, Congress in 2005 passed the new Central American Free Trade Agreement (CAFTA), which extended NAFTA into five Central American countries and the Dominican Republic. —AM

"Free Trade on Trial: Ten Years of NAFTA"
by Staff Writers
Economist, **January 3, 2004**

From the start, the North American Free-Trade Agreement was bitterly controversial in all three of the countries taking part—the United States, Canada and Mexico. Its terms, which went into effect on January 1st 1994, were argued over line by line: despite its name, the agreement fell far short of scrapping all trade restrictions, and the fine print of the various exemptions and exclusions gave rise to heated argument. More than this, the agreement was attacked as bad in principle. Everybody recognized that NAFTA was an extraordinarily bold attempt to accelerate economic integration—or, as critics put it, an experiment in reckless globalization. As such, they said, it would destroy jobs, make the poor worse off and start an environmental race to the bottom.

Equally, advocates of the agreement made some bold claims about the good it would bring. Far from destroying jobs, it would create lots of new and better ones; incomes would rise and the poor would benefit proportionately; growth would accelerate and, to the extent that this posed environmental challenges, extra resources would be available to meet them.

Unsurprisingly, a mere ten years' experience has settled few of these quarrels. Today, most trade economists read the evidence as saying that NAFTA has worked: intra-area trade and foreign investment have expanded greatly. Trade skeptics and anti-globalists look at the same history and feel no less vindicated. Look at Mexico's growth since 1994, they say—dismal for much of the period. Look at the contraction of manufacturing employment in the United States. As for the environment, go to the places south of the border where the *maquiladoras* cluster, and take a deep breath.

Politically, the skeptics, ten years on, can fairly claim victory. NAFTA is unpopular in all three countries. In Mexico, which stood to gain most from freer trade (since its barriers were so much higher at the outset) and which has indeed benefited greatly according to most economic appraisals, the agreement is widely regarded as having been useless or worse. In a poll conducted at the end of 2002 by Ipsos-Reid for the Woodrow Wilson Centre in Washington, only 29% of Mexicans interviewed said that NAFTA has benefited Mexico; 33% thought that it had hurt the country and 33% said that it had made no difference. In all three countries, the perceived results of NAFTA seem to have eroded support for further trade liberalization.

NAFTA's champions are partly to blame for this: they oversold their case. It was never plausible, for instance, to expect that NAFTA would be a net creator of jobs. Trade policy is not a driver of overall employment; it affects the pattern of jobs, rather than the total number. To the extent that NAFTA succeeds in stimulating trade and cross-border flows of investment, jobs in each member country are created in some industries and destroyed in others. This was bound to be a painful process for some, even if it succeeded in making the member countries' economies more efficient overall, and hence in raising average incomes. Here was another instance of false advertising: NAFTA was never going to be, as some enthusiasts claimed, a win-win proposition for all of North America's citizens, even if all three countries could hope to gain in the aggregate.

Yes, It Worked

So far as its economic effects are concerned, the right question to ask of NAFTA is simply whether it indeed succeeded in stimulating trade and investment. The answer is clear: it did. In 1990 the United States' exports to, and imports from, Canada and Mexico accounted for about a quarter of its trade; now they account for about a third. That is a dramatic switch, especially when one notes that the United States' non-NAFTA trade has itself grown strongly over the period. There is plenty of economic evidence to suggest that expanded trade, as a rule, raises incomes and future rates of growth. So it is pretty clear that NAFTA achieved as much as one could sensibly have expected it to achieve.

Why then is the agreement so widely regarded by non-economists as a failure? The answer lies partly in the interplay of politics and economics, and accordingly is different in each of the member countries. But one theme is common to all three: a tendency to blame NAFTA in particular, and international integration in general, for every economic disappointment of the past ten years, however tenuous the connection may be.

Debate in the United States has been preoccupied by fears over loss of jobs—by the "giant sucking sound" of work moving south, in Ross Perot's phrase from the early 1990s. A variety of estimates of NAFTA's direct effect on American labor have been made—with job losses running as high, according to one disputed study, as 110,000 a year between 1994 and 2000.

But, as already noted, direct losses do not tell the whole story: changing the pattern of employment is after all one of the reasons for promoting trade. So long as lost jobs are balanced by new ones, the overall effect on employment will be small. As Gary Hufbauer and Jeffrey Schott of the Institute for International Economics point out, between 1994 and 2000 the United States economy created more than 2 million new jobs a year. Manufacturing employment has dwindled (with NAFTA as one relatively minor cause among many); jobs in other industries have more than made up the losses. And since the mid-1990s, at any rate, the great majority of new jobs created have paid above-median wages.

Against this background, even NAFTA's highest estimated direct losses can hardly be regarded as crippling. America's evident disenchantment with liberal trade has less to do with the economic depredations of the 1990s—when the economy boomed, in fact—than with a political failure to make the case for free trade against its increasingly vocal and well-organized opponents.

In Canada, initial concerns were less to do with the flight of low-skilled manufacturing jobs, because trade with Mexico seemed a less pressing issue than it was for the United States, and more to do with other sorts of international competition. As it turned out, Canadian unemployment fell markedly during the 1990s (from 11% of the labor force in 1993 to 7% in 2000). The main fear, instead, was that closer integration with the American economy would threaten Canada's European-style social-welfare model, either by leading certain practices and policies (such as the generous minimum wage) to be regarded as directly uncompetitive, or else by pressing down on the country's base of corporate and personal taxes, thereby starving public-spending programs of resources.

Canadian public spending was indeed squeezed somewhat during the 1990s—not because NAFTA eroded the tax base, but because public borrowing had reached an unsustainable level of 8% of GDP in the early 1990s. The problem was successfully addressed: Canada has lately run a budget surplus. Despite the fiscal retrenchment, and despite NAFTA, its social-welfare model stands intact, and in sharp contrast with that of the United States. The fact is, most Canadians are willing to pay the higher taxes that are required to finance generous public services (including universal health care). As long as this remains true, NAFTA poses no threat to the Canadian way of life.

Down South

What about Mexico? The very point of NAFTA, to listen to some of its advocates, was to destroy the Mexican way of life—and replace it with something better. The overall verdict on NAFTA rests heavily on whether the pact proved a success for the country it was bound to affect most. NAFTA was never going to have much impact on the huge economy of the United States. But as recently as the mid-1980s Mexico was still an almost completely closed economy. For Mexico, NAFTA promised to be revolutionary.

Unfortunately, soon after NAFTA came into effect, the country was overwhelmed by a largely unrelated economic shock, the Tequila crisis of 1994–95. Huge capital inflows into the country in the early 1990s were followed by rapid outflows towards the end of 1994, causing the peso to plunge. The authorities were forced to float the currency on December 20th of that year, and before long it had lost nearly half of its value against the dollar.

The financial system collapsed, with many banks going under as years of bad loans were exposed. In the end, at huge cost, the government had to bail out the banks. The repercussions of the Tequila crisis for Mexico were immense. The banks, for instance, have still not fully recovered, and the subsequent lack of credit and financial services does much to explain the anemic performance of Mexico's domestic economy over the past decade. All this makes judging the effects of NAFTA very difficult.

Take real wages. Although Mexican workers have managed impressive gains in productivity over the past ten years to compete with America and Canada, real wages have not kept pace. This allows NAFTA's critics to argue that the typical Mexican has not benefited from the treaty as he should have done, and that big business has creamed off most of the profits.

The truth is different. The Tequila crisis led to an immediate fall of about 20% in Mexican wages (more in dollar terms), while productivity kept going up. So although real wages have been rising ever since the country began to recover in 1996, they are only just reaching their levels of before the crisis. The lasting influence of higher productivity on wages may not be clear for another decade, when the effects of the Tequila crisis have fully faded away. That said, the country recovered much more quickly from the Tequila crisis than from its previous financial crises in 1982 and 1986—and this was indeed mainly due to NAFTA. Speedily arranged help from Bill Clinton's administration spurred the strong recovery. That aid sprang from America's desire not to let its new partner go under.

The closeness of the link to America, the destination of almost 90% of Mexican exports, is of course a disadvantage when America goes into recession, as it did in 2001. Mexico lost thousands of export jobs in that downswing. On the other hand, NAFTA has insulated Mexico against the financial instability that swept through Argentina, Brazil and other parts of South America in the first years of the new century. It has given Mexico an investment-grade credit rating, and allowed it to issue—almost uniquely in Latin America—very long-term local-currency bonds and mortgage-backed securities. Investors now think of Mexico more as a North American than a Latin American country.

Former President Carlos Salinas de Gortari embraced NAFTA mostly to attract more foreign investment and to boost the *maquiladora* manufacturers (set up in 1965 to allow tariff-free import of materials for assembly and re-export to the United States). Mexico's trade has surged, especially with the United States. In 2002 it totaled $250 billion, and the country's traditional deficit with its northern neighbor has been converted into a surplus in every year of NAFTA membership.

After 1994 foreign direct investment also shot up. NAFTA was designed to make investors feel more legally secure, and foreign companies duly poured in to take advantage of Mexico's closeness to the world's wealthiest market. The rise in export manufacturing also greatly reduced the country's dependence on the volatile price of oil. Moreover, NAFTA jobs in export businesses have usually been good ones, paying on average substantially more than jobs in the rest of the economy.

It hardly needs saying, however, that Mexico has no shortage of problems that NAFTA has so far failed to solve. One is the challenge of providing decently paid work for all those who need it. The chief symptom of the failure to do that, of course, is the continuing outflow of migrants.

The biggest pressure on emigration, in turn, is the crisis in the countryside. The traditional Mexican farmer had about eight hectares of his own land and some communal land for livestock. This made his family self-sufficient in everything from maize and beans to meat and milk. Even before NAFTA this traditional rural economy was disappearing, as demographic pressure caused the land to be subdivided, and many *campesinos* now eke out a living year by year, ever on the edge of disaster. "If the weather does not help us, we are completely lost," says Dionisio Garcia, who farms a smallholding in the southern state of Tlaxcala.

Most of Mr. Garcia's colleagues have simply given up. He estimates that up to 90% of the heads of families in his area now spend at least six months of the year working in Canada or the United States. "What they earn there in four months, we don't earn here in a year," he says. They are part of an estimated 1.3 million people who have left the land since 1994. The young, besides, are no longer much interested in making a living from the land; they are going off to drive taxis in the city, or to sell air-conditioners.

Mr. Garcia says that he can no longer sell his surplus maize to Mexican wholesalers because he has been undercut by cheaper and better American imports. For him, NAFTA and free trade have been "totally bad." And yet trade in Mexico's two staples, maize and beans, is still not free; the last tariffs will remain until 2008.

The flood of corn from America's mid-west is the most hated aspect of NAFTA for Mexicans. The government argues that it has to import so much because Mexico's small farmers cannot feed all Mexicans, let alone turn a profit. But critics allege that Americans are selling so cheap that they are, in effect, dumping the stuff. Besides, they receive vast subsidies from their government. NAFTA explicitly pledges to eliminate these, but it has not done so yet.

Some Mexican farmers have shown that they can make a good living under NAFTA. Export earnings from horticulture have tripled since 1994, to over $3.5 billion; exports of fresh vegetables have risen by 80% and fresh fruit by 90%. If farmers can exploit local conditions and invest in a crop that can be exported during American or European winters, they can make money. The star performer is the Hass avocado from the state of Michoacán, in the west of Mexico, where the climate is mild and the soil fertile. Before NAFTA, the United States banned it because of infestation by insects. After a clean-up and monitoring operation, supervised under NAFTA rules, avocados from

Michoacán were accepted into most states of America in 1997. Exports have increased from 6,000 tons to 30,000 tons a year.

Overall, though, Mexico continues to rely on low-cost assembly, and the advantage of preferential entry into the American market. Increasingly, other countries offer cheaper labor. With China's accession to the World Trade Organization, Mexico has already lost much of the advantage that NAFTA gave it. Many Mexicans still think that a reviving American economy, by itself, can buoy their own. But in the next upswing, as America deepens its trade links with other states, this may prove untrue.

NAFTA alone has not been enough to modernize the country or guarantee prosperity. It was never reasonable to suppose that it would be—though that did not stop many of its advocates saying so. NAFTA has spurred trade for all its members. That is a good thing. But trade can do only so much. Sadly, successive Mexican governments have failed to deal with the problems—corruption, poor education, red tape, crumbling infrastructure, lack of credit and a puny tax base— that have prevented Mexicans and foreign investors alike from exploiting the openings which freer trade afforded. Don't blame NAFTA for that.

Like many multinational corporations, Nike, the sports and fitness giant, contracts with factories in countries such as Vietnam and Indonesia where labor and production costs are low. In 2004, Nike had more than 660,000 contract manufacturing workers in more than 900 factories in more than fifty countries. In the mid-1990s, critics of Nike claimed

that its contract workers were underpaid and exploited, while consumers paid high prices for shoes with the Nike "swoosh." New York Times *columnist Bob Herbert wrote about an Indonesian factory where workers were fired for demanding the minimum wage of $1.25 a day. Nike chief executive Philip H. Knight responded that Nike paid, on average, double the minimum wage to its contract workers, and that Nike would be "out of business" if it did not produce in low-income societies like its competitors.*

Debate continues over the obligations of multinational companies in countries with low wages and living standards. Swedish writer Johan Norberg, a proponent of free trade, argues that Nike offers opportunity to people who might otherwise not have a job. —AM

"The Noble Feat of Nike"
by Johan Norberg
Spectator, June 7, 2003

Nike. It means victory. It also means a type of expensive gym shoe. In the minds of the anti-globalisation movement, it stands for both at once. Nike stands for the victory of a Western footwear company over the poor and dispossessed. Spongy, smelly, hungered after by kids across the world, Nike is the symbol of the unacceptable triumph of global capital.

A Nike is a shoe that simultaneously kicks people out of jobs in the West, and tramples on the poor in the Third World. Sold for 100 times more than the wages of the peons who make them, Nike shoes are hate-objects more potent, in the eyes of the protesters at this week's G8 riots, than McDonald's hamburgers. If you want to be trendy these days, you don't wear Nikes; you boycott them.

So I was interested to hear someone not only praising Nike sweatshops, but also claiming that Nike is an example of a good and responsible business. That someone was the ruling Communist party of Vietnam.

Today Nike has almost four times more workers in Vietnam than in the United States. I traveled to Ho Chi Minh to examine the effects of multinational corporations on poor countries. Nike being the most notorious multinational villain, and Vietnam being a dictatorship with a documented lack of free speech, the operation is supposed to be a classic of conscience-free capitalist oppression.

In truth the work does look tough, and the conditions grim, if we compare Vietnamese factories with what we have back home. But that's not the comparison these workers make. They compare the work at Nike with the way they lived before, or the way their parents or neighbors still work. And the facts are revealing. The average pay at a Nike factory close to Ho Chi Minh is $54 a month, almost three times the minimum wage for a state-owned enterprise.

Ten years ago, when Nike was established in Vietnam, the workers had to walk to the factories, often for many miles. After three years on Nike wages, they could afford bicycles. Another three years later, they could afford scooters, so they all take the scooters to work (and if you go there, beware; they haven't really decided on which side of the road to drive). Today, the first workers can afford to buy a car.

But when I talk to a young Vietnamese woman, Tsi-Chi, at the factory, it is not the wages she is most happy about.

Sure, she makes five times more than she did, she earns more than her husband, and she can now afford to build an extension to her house. But the most important thing, she says, is that she doesn't have to work outdoors on a farm any more. For me, a Swede with only three months of summer, this sounds bizarre. Surely working conditions under the blue sky must be superior to those in a sweatshop? But then I am naively Eurocentric. Farming means 10 to 14 hours a day in the burning sun or the intensive rain, in rice fields with water up to your ankles and insects in your face. Even a Swede would prefer working nine to five in a clean, air-conditioned factory.

Furthermore, the Nike job comes with a regular wage, with free or subsidized meals, free medical services and training and education. The most persistent demand Nike hears from the workers is for an expansion of the factories so that their relatives can be offered a job as well.

These facts make Nike sound more like Santa Claus than Scrooge. But corporations such as Nike don't bring these benefits and wages because they are generous. It is not altruism that is at work here; it is globalization. With their investments in poor countries, multinationals bring new machinery, better technology, new management skills and production ideas, a larger market and the education of their workers. That is exactly what raises productivity. And if you increase productivity—the amount a worker can produce—you can also increase his wage.

Nike is not the accidental good guy. On average, multi-nationals in the least developed countries pay twice as much as domestic companies in the same line of business. If you get to work for an American multinational in a low-income country, you get eight times the average income. If this is exploitation, then the problem in our world is that the poor countries aren't sufficiently exploited.

The effect on local business is profound: "Before I visit some foreign factory, especially like Nike, we have a question. Why do the foreign factories here work well and produce much more?" That was what Mr. Kiet, the owner of a local shoe factory who visited Nike to learn how he could be just as successful at attracting workers, told me: "And I recognize that productivity does not only come from machinery but also from satisfaction of the worker. So for the future factory we should concentrate on our working conditions."

If I was an antiglobalist, I would stop complaining about Nike's bad wages. If there is a problem, it is that the wages are too high, so that they are almost luring doctors and teachers away from their important jobs.

But—happily—I don't think even that is a realistic threat. With growing productivity it will also be possible to invest in education and healthcare for Vietnam. Since 1990, when the Vietnamese communists began to liberalize the economy, exports of coffee, rice, clothes and footwear have surged, the economy has doubled, and poverty has been halved. Nike and Coca-Cola triumphed where American bombs failed. They have made Vietnam capitalist.

I asked the young Nike worker Tsi-Chi what her hopes were for her son's future. A generation ago, she would have had to put him to work on the farm from an early age. But Tsi-Chi told me she wants to give him a good education, so that he can become a doctor. That's one of the most impressive develop-ments since Vietnam's economy was opened up. In ten years

2.2 million children have gone from child labor to education. It would be extremely interesting to hear an antiglobalist explain to Tsi-Chi why it is important for Westerners to boycott Nike, so that she loses her job, and has to go back into farming, and has to send her son to work.

The European Left used to listen to the Vietnamese communists when they brought only misery and starvation to their population. Shouldn't they listen to the Vietnamese now, when they have found a way to improve people's lives? The party officials have been convinced by Nike that ruthless multinational capitalists are better than the state at providing workers with high wages and a good and healthy workplace. How long will it take for our own anticapitalists to learn that lesson?

The antiglobalization movement caught the world's attention when protesters flooded Seattle to disrupt the World Trade Organization (WTO) meeting in 1999. Some 600 people were arrested, widespread property damage was incurred, and the meeting was shut down. Since Seattle, protesters have turned out to disrupt meetings of the World Bank, the International Monetary Fund (IMF), the WTO, and the G8, a group of the wealthiest nations. The diverse coalition of students, labor rights advocates, environmentalists, and others is pushing for changes in these institutions. Globalization has worsened poverty and injustice, increased inequality, and hurt the environment, the activists say. They demand more debt relief, international aid, and trade justice for poor nations. The protesters are not against global ties and

opened borders. "We want to globalize equity not poverty, solidarity not anti-sociality, diversity not conformity, democracy not subordination, and ecological balance not suicidal rapaciousness," stated writer and antiglobalization activist Michael Albert. Their voices have definitely been heard; the World Bank and other institutions are tackling many of these difficult issues. —*AM*

"Police Haul Hundreds to Jail; Downtown Seattle Declared a Restricted Zone"
by David Postman, Jack Broom, and Florangela Davila
Seattle Times, December 1, 1999

SEATTLE—Police and about 1,000 protesters continued their battle for the streets of Seattle Wednesday, even after a zone of more than 50 blocks was declared off-limits to demonstrators and was surrounded by police, state troopers, King County sheriff's deputies and National Guardsmen, many wearing riot gear.

Despite those measures, hundreds of protesters managed to get inside the restricted zone, and at least 225 were arrested, most of them after protesting near Westlake Center.

They were placed on buses and taken to the former Sand Point naval station for booking. Most were docile while others shouted, "Down with the WTO!" or "I love America!"

The restricted zone—bounded by Boren Avenue, Seneca Street, Fourth Avenue and Lenora Street—will remain off-limits to demonstrations until the close of the World Trade Organization conference Friday.

As police made arrests and moved to other areas in the zone, about 1,000 people moved up Pine Street to Sixth Avenue, where about 100 police met them and told them to leave the area or chemical agents would be used.

When crowds grew large, police became aggressive and broke them up; in other places, protesters were allowed to go virtually unimpeded, blocking traffic with no police presence.

At one intersection along the perimeter Wednesday morning, a deputy shouted at a group of guardsmen: "You're letting them through. Don't let them through unless they show you their ID."

"It's nothing personal," a patrol officer told several others trying to enter a checkpoint, "but you have to have a legitimate WTO pass. Those are the rules for this post."

Other people were being let in after displaying business cards or other identification showing they worked inside the restricted area.

The American Civil Liberties Union of Washington was preparing to seek a temporary restraining order against the restriction, calling it "an overreaction to the day's events."

Police had hoped to allow protests and the WTO meetings to occur at the same time, Assistant Seattle Police Chief Ed Joiner said at a news conference Wednesday morning. "Clearly, in hindsight, the approach we used did not work. If we had known what was going to occur, we would have taken a different position in the first place."

The announcement of the restricted area came after one of the largest demonstrations in Seattle's history turned ugly Tuesday.

Up to 35,000 protesters took to the streets to protest the WTO. In their attempt to stop the conference, they formed human blockades, sat cross-legged in intersections and chained themselves to scaffolding with bicycle locks. They managed to tie up streets around the Washington State Convention and Trade Center, where many WTO meetings are being held, prompting the cancellation of the conference's opening ceremony.

While most remained peaceful, pockets of protesters became violent—breaking windows, spray-painting buildings and throwing cans and bottles.

Police, trying to open up a route for delegates to get to the conference, responded with pepper spray and rubber bullets.

Joiner said 68 protesters were arrested before Wednesday's restriction.

King County prosecutors said they will ask that bail be set at $25,000 for 10 people accused of breaking windows, looting or assault.

More than two dozen protesters, three police officers and two delegates were treated at hospitals for minor injuries. One demonstrator suffered a broken ankle.

"I'm anticipating much greater calm in the streets today," said Police Chief Norm Stamper as he watched protesters being arrested. "We have more reinforcements."

"I'm not going to try to put a positive spin" on Tuesday's events, Stamper said at a news conference Wednesday, saying it's anguishing to drive down the streets of Seattle and witness graffiti, trash, boarded-up windows and even fires. "That's not a pretty sight for a city we have all come to know and love."

But he praised his officers' handling of the protests Tuesday, saying that "against all odds, our people responded very, very effectively."

At Wednesday's news conference, Stamper also said that nobody but police would be allowed to possess or use gas masks within the restricted zone. Police in and around the zone told journalists the same thing, seizing the mask of a news reporter.

Part of Wednesday's extreme security was due to the fact that President Clinton arrived in town for the WTO conference. "We certainly would want to do what we can to protect our president," Stamper said.

Clinton arrived just hours after Seattle Mayor Paul Schell declared a civil emergency and Gov. Gary Locke called on the National Guard to relieve weary police.

Mass Arrests

Wednesday morning, as protesters attempted to get inside the restricted area, police at Lenora Street and Westlake Avenue arrested them and loaded them onto Metro buses, filling one bus and about a third of an articulated bus, whose passengers had been unloaded by the police.

At Westlake Park, police filled two more buses with protesters. The group there had brought protest signs and handcuffs to chain themselves together, but at the perimeter police searched them and seized the signs and handcuffs.

"Stay calm. If they bust us here this will be known as Seattle's Tiananmen Square," said a man who goes by the single name Asante and is affiliated with the Direct Action Network, a group that has coordinated some of the protests.

He urged the protesters to be peaceful and said they should leave if they couldn't be.

Seattle police Capt. Jim Pugel said the protesters were being arrested for pedestrian interference and refusal to disperse. He said they were blocking the sidewalk.

"Our intent is to keep the peace in the entire city of Seattle," he said.

In one sweep of arrests at Westlake Park, police took a Canadian radio announcer in the middle of a live broadcast. Other broadcasters identified him as Ted Field of Vancouver station CKNW.

At Fourth and Pine, double amputee Sha King shouted at police as they went by, "Shoot the bullets, shoot the gas. Get these people off the streets. What are you afraid of?"

"The protesters are not doing anything for the homeless," said a street person in the area.

Schell said police were restrained in their actions Tuesday largely to ensure that law-abiding demonstrators were not hurt.

Wednesday's actions would be different because protesters have been warned not to come into the area, Schell said. "Our responses will be swift. Anyone who engages in criminal conduct will be dealt with appropriately."

Schell said he was proud of the vast majority of the protesters who acted peacefully Tuesday, saying some even volunteered to help clean up the city overnight.

Wednesday's police response is more in keeping with the police actions in other cities, said Joiner, the assistant chief. Seattle had hoped to handle it in a more open fashion, he said, by allowing demonstrators into the general area of the event. But it didn't work.

With the restricted zone in place, delegates and others were able to get easily into Wednesday's events at the WTO conference after passing through a checkpoint and metal detectors.

"This is a lot more calm," said Kathy Schrier, a high-school journalism teacher who attended the conference with 20 high-school journalism students. "Yesterday, we had a couple of people trapped in here who couldn't get out, people outside who couldn't get in and a couple of people sort of trapped by the human chain."

Two of the students were hit by tear gas as they attempted to photograph the demonstration.

State of Emergency

During the height of Tuesday's demonstrations, people calling themselves anarchists and dressed in black roamed the streets, smashing windows at Nike Town, Planet Hollywood, Nordstrom and a half-dozen other stores.

Graffiti was spray-painted on scores of cars, buildings and street signs. Windows at a Starbucks at Sixth Avenue and Pine Street were smashed and a Starbucks at Sixth and Stewart Street was looted. Because of several assaults on bus drivers during the protests, Metro bus service was suspended downtown.

Other protesters tried to stop the vandals but had no success. The violence diverted attention from the vast majority of protesters who not only were peaceful but attempted to enforce the peace among fellow demonstrators.

"I am so disappointed how this turned out. We had weeks of training how to do this correctly. It was supposed to be peaceful," said Catherine Ahern, a protester from Seattle.

"It's been completely destroyed. Our message is not going to get out and I'm so mad."

Tuesday afternoon, Schell declared a civil emergency, authorizing a curfew from 7 p.m. [PT] Tuesday until 7:30 a.m. [PT] Wednesday covering most of downtown from Denny to Yesler and from Interstate 5 to the waterfront.

Police then made their move to begin clearing downtown.

Block by block, officers fired canisters of gas into the crowds with a terrifying boom. Then they shot rubber bullets into the backs of protesters even as they ran away.

As darkness fell, police drove protesters out of downtown and into surrounding neighborhoods, with large numbers swarming Capitol Hill.

As police crept up Capitol Hill, pushing protesters back with rubber bullets and gas, the shouts became less and less about the WTO and more a turf battle telling police to "get off our hill."

By midnight, officers boarded a bus and left the area. The protesters left shortly after.

Behind the protests is a concern about WTO authority to override national laws found to impede trade. Protesters say the trade organization threatens U.S. environmental laws and sets back human-rights initiatives. And labor groups complain the WTO allows jobs to be exported to countries with less stringent workplace rules.

CHAPTER TWO

PRODUCTION, DISTRIBUTION, AND CONSUMPTION: HOW GLOBALIZATION AFFECTS THE WORLD ECONOMY

By 2003, the exporting of American jobs overseas had expanded to include high-paying white-collar jobs, not just manufacturing jobs. Access to the Internet, liberal trade rules, and a ready pool of educated workers allowed industries to set up offices in other countries. This phenomenon—known as offshoring—sent waves of panic through many professions, including software engineering, finance, and even medicine. Offshoring works best for jobs that are based on information, use the computer, and do not require face-to-face contact. The software industry was the first to move to foreign locations like Bangalore, India, but finance, publishing, radiology, and other information industries have followed.

This Business Week *story created a stir: the middle class had only begun to realize that a globalized economy could put their jobs at risk. Still, many economists say that offshoring will not lead to permanent job loss, but rather to a new mix of occupations in the U.S. economy—it will just take time. —AM*

From "The New Global Job Shift"
by Pete Engardio, Aaron Bernstein, and Manjeet Kripalani with Frederik Balfour in Manila, Brian Grow in Atlanta, and Jay Greene in Seattle
Business Week, February 3, 2003

The sense of resignation inside Bank of America (BAC) is clear from the e-mail dispatch. "The handwriting is on the wall," writes a veteran information-technology specialist who says he has been warned not to talk to the press. Three years ago, the Charlotte (N.C.)-based bank needed IT talent so badly it had to outbid rivals. But last fall, his entire 15-engineer team was told their jobs "wouldn't last through September." In the past year, BofA has slashed 3,700 of its 25,000 tech and back-office jobs. An additional 1,000 will go by March.

Corporate downsizings, of course, are part of the ebb and flow of business. These layoffs, though, aren't just happening because demand has dried up. Ex-BofA managers and contractors say one-third of those jobs are headed to India, where work that costs $100 an hour in the U.S. gets done for $20. Many former BofA workers are returning to college to learn new software skills. Some are getting real estate licenses. BofA acknowledges it will outsource up to 1,100 jobs to Indian companies this year, but it insists not all India-bound jobs are leading to layoffs.

Cut to India. In dazzling new technology parks rising on the dusty outskirts of the major cities, no one's talking about job losses. Inside Infosys Technologies Ltd.'s (INFY) impeccably landscaped 22-hectare campus in Bangalore, 250 engineers develop IT applications for BofA. Elsewhere, Infosys staffers process home loans for Greenpoint Mortgage of Novato, Calif. Near Bangalore's airport, at the offices of Wipro Ltd. (WIT), five radiologists interpret 30 CT scans a day for Massachusetts General Hospital. Not far away, 26-year-old engineer Dharin Shah talks excitedly about his $10,000-a-year job designing third-generation mobile-phone chips, as sun pours through a skylight at the Texas Instrument Inc. (TXN) research center. Five years ago, an engineer like Shah would have made a beeline for Silicon Valley. Now, he says, "The sky is the limit here."

About 1,600 km north, on an old flour mill site outside New Delhi, all four floors of Wipro Spectramind Ltd.'s sandstone-and-glass building are buzzing at midnight with 2,500 young college-educated men and women. They are processing claims for a major U.S. insurance company and providing help-desk support for a big U.S. Internet service provider—all at a cost up to 60% lower than in the U.S. Seven Wipro Spectramind staff with PhDs in molecular biology sift through scientific research for Western pharmaceutical companies. Behind glass-framed doors, Wipro voice coaches drill staff on how to speak American English. U.S. customers like a familiar accent on the other end of the line.

Cut again to Manila, Shanghai, Budapest, or San José, Costa Rica. These cities—and dozens more across the developing world—have become the new back offices for Corporate America, Japan Inc., and Europe GmbH. Never heard of Balazs Zimay? He's a Budapest architect—and just might help design your future dream house. The name SGV & Co. probably means nothing to you. But this Manila firm's accountants may crunch the numbers the next time Ernst & Young International audits your company. Even Bulgaria, Romania, and South Africa, which have a lot of educated people but remain economic backwaters, are tapping the global market for services.

It's globalization's next wave—and one of the biggest trends reshaping the global economy. The first wave started two decades ago with the exodus of jobs making shoes, cheap electronics, and toys to developing countries. After that, simple service work, like processing credit-card receipts, and mind-numbing digital toil, like writing software code, began fleeing high-cost countries.

Now, all kinds of knowledge work can be done almost anywhere. "You will see an explosion of work going overseas," says Forrester Research Inc. analyst John C. McCarthy. He goes so far as to predict at least 3.3 million white-collar jobs and $136 billion in wages will shift from the U.S. to low-cost countries by 2015. Europe is joining the trend, too. British banks like HSBC Securities Inc. (HBC) have huge back offices in China and India; French companies are using call centers in Mauritius; and German multinationals from Siemens (SI) to roller-bearings maker INA-Schaeffler are hiring in Russia, the Baltics, and Eastern Europe.

The driving forces are digitization, the Internet, and high-speed data networks that girdle the globe. These days, tasks such as drawing up detailed architectural blueprints, slicing and dicing a company's financial disclosures, or designing a revolutionary microprocessor can easily be performed overseas. That's why Intel Inc. (INTC) and Texas Instruments Inc. are furiously hiring Indian and Chinese engineers, many with graduate degrees, to design chip circuits. Dutch consumer-electronics giant Philips (PHG) has shifted research and development on most televisions, cell phones, and audio products to Shanghai. In a recent PowerPoint presentation, Microsoft Corp. (MSFT) Senior Vice-President Brian Valentine—the No. 2 exec in the company's Windows unit—urged managers to "pick something to move offshore today." In India, said the briefing, you can get "quality work at 50% to 60% of the cost. That's two heads for the price of one."

Even Wall Street jobs paying $80,000 and up are getting easier to transfer. Brokerages like Lehman Brothers Inc. (LEH) and Bear, Stearns & Co. (BSC), for example, are starting to use Indian financial analysts for number-crunching work. "A basic business tenet is that things go to the areas where there is the best cost of production," says Ann Livermore, head of services at Hewlett-Packard Co. (HPQ), which has 3,300 software engineers in India. "Now you're going to see the same trends in services that happened in manufacturing."

The rise of a globally integrated knowledge economy is a blessing for developing nations. What it means for the U.S. skilled labor force is less clear. At the least, many white-collar workers may be headed for a tough readjustment. The unprecedented hiring binge in Asia, Eastern Europe, and Latin America comes at a time when companies from Wall Street to Silicon Valley are downsizing at home. In Silicon Valley, employment in the IT sector is down by 20% since early 2001, according to the nonprofit group Joint Venture Silicon Valley.

Should the West panic? It's too early to tell. Obviously, the bursting of the tech bubble and Wall Street's woes are chiefly behind the layoffs. Also, any impact of offshore hiring is hard to measure, since so far a tiny portion of U.S. white-collar work has jumped overseas. For security and practical reasons, corporations are likely to keep crucial R&D and the bulk of back-office operations close to home. Many jobs can't go anywhere because they require face-to-face contact with customers. Americans will continue to deliver medical care, negotiate deals, audit local companies, and wage legal battles. Talented, innovative people will adjust as they always have.

Indeed, a case can be made that the U.S. will see a net gain from this shift—as with previous globalization waves. In the 1990s, Corporate America had to import hundreds of thousands of immigrants to ease engineering shortages. Now, by sending routine service and engineering tasks to nations with a surplus of educated workers, the U.S. labor force and capital can be redeployed to higher-value industries and cutting-edge R&D. "Silicon Valley doesn't need to have all the tech development in the world," says Doug Henton, president of Collaborative Economics in Mountview, Calif. "We need very good-paying jobs. Any R&D that is routine can probably go." Silicon Valley types already talk about the next wave of U.S. innovation coming from the fusion of software, nanotech, and life sciences.

Globalization should also keep services prices in check, just as it did with clothes, appliances, and home tools when manufacturing went offshore. Companies will be able to keep shaving overhead costs and improving efficiency. "Our comparative advantage may shift to other fields," says City University of New York economist Robert E. Lipsey, a trade specialist. "And if productivity is high, then the U.S. will maintain a high standard of living." By spurring economic development in nations such as India, meanwhile, U.S. companies will have bigger foreign markets for their goods and services.

For companies adept at managing a global workforce, the benefits can be huge. Sure, entrusting administration and R&D to far-flung foreigners sounds risky. But Corporate America already has become comfortable hiring outside companies to handle everything from product design and tech support to employee benefits. Letting such work cross national boundaries isn't a radical leap. Now, American Express (AXP), Dell Computer (DELL), Eastman Kodak (EK), and other companies can offer round-the-clock customer care while keeping costs in check. What's more, immigrant Asian engineers in the U.S. labs of TI, IBM (IBM), and Intel for decades have played a big, hidden role in American tech breakthroughs. The difference now is that Indian and Chinese engineers are managing R&D teams in their home countries. General Electric Co. (GE), for example, employs some 6,000 scientists and engineers in 10 foreign countries. GE Medical Services integrates magnet, flat-panel, and diagnostic imaging technologies from labs in China, Israel, Hungary, France, and India in everything from its new X-ray devices to $1 million CT scanners. "The real advantage is that we can tap the world's best talent," says GE Medical Global Supply Chain Vice-President Dee Miller.

That's the good side of the coming realignment. There are hazards as well. During previous go-global drives, many companies ended up repatriating manufacturing and design work because they felt they were losing control of core businesses or found them too hard to coordinate. In a recent Gartner Inc. survey of 900 big U.S. companies that outsource

IT work offshore, a majority complained of difficulty communicating and meeting deadlines. As a result, predicts Gartner Inc. Research Director Frances Karamouzis, many newcomers will stumble in the first few years as they begin using offshore service workers.

A thornier question: What happens if all those displaced white-collar workers can't find greener pastures? Sure, tech specialists, payroll administrators, and Wall Street analysts will land new jobs. But will they be able to make the same money as before? It's possible that lower salaries for skilled work will outweigh the gains in corporate efficiency. "If foreign countries specialize in high-skilled areas where we have an advantage, we could be worse off," says Harvard University economist Robert Z. Lawrence, a prominent free-trade advocate. "I still have faith that globalization will make us better off, but it's no more than faith . . ."

———————■———————

Antiglobalization protesters may be on to something, writes Joseph S. Nye Jr., a former U.S. assistant defense secretary and the dean of Harvard's Kennedy School of Government from 1995 to 2004. While he may not always agree with their tactics, Nye acknowledges that the protesters' criticism of multinational institutions should be taken seriously. The charge that openness and democracy are lacking in the institutions that wield the money and power fueling globalization is legitimate, writes Nye. He urges the multinational institutions to become more accountable and forthright in their processes. He also suggests that they become more responsible to the people they serve. —AM

"Globalization's Democratic Deficit: How to Make International Institutions More Accountable"
by Joseph S. Nye Jr.
Foreign Policy, July/August 2001

Seattle; Washington, D.C.; Prague; Quebec City. It is becoming difficult for international economic organizations to meet without attracting crowds of protesters decrying globalization. These protesters are a diverse lot, coming mainly from rich countries, and their coalition has not always been internally consistent. They have included trade unionists worried about losing jobs and students who want to help the underdeveloped world gain them, environmentalists concerned about ecological degradation and anarchists who object to all forms of international regulation. Some protesters claim to represent poor countries but simultaneously defend agricultural protectionism in wealthy countries. Some reject corporate capitalism, whereas others accept the benefits of international markets but worry that globalization is destroying democracy.

Of all their complaints, this last concern is key. Protest organizers such as Lori Wallach attributed half the success of the Seattle coalition to "the notion that the democracy deficit in the global economy is neither necessary nor acceptable." For globalization's supporters, accordingly, finding some way to address its perceived democratic deficit should become a high priority.

It's a Small World

Globalization, defined as networks of interdependence at worldwide distances, is not new. Nor is it just economic.

Markets have spread and tied people together, but environmental, military, social, and political interdependence have also increased. If the current political backlash against globalization were to lead to a rash of protectionist policies, it might slow or even reverse the world's economic integration—as has happened at times in the past—even as global warming or the spread of the AIDS virus continued apace. It would be ironic if current protests curtailed the positive aspects of globalization while leaving the negative dimensions untouched.

Markets have unequal effects, and the inequality they produce can have powerful political consequences. But the cliché that markets always make the rich richer and the poor poorer is simply not true. Globalization, for example, has improved the lot of hundreds of millions of poor people around the world. Poverty can be reduced even when inequality increases. And in some cases inequality can even decrease. The economic gap between South Korea and industrialized countries, for example, has diminished in part because of global markets. No poor country, meanwhile, has ever become rich by isolating itself from global markets, although North Korea and Myanmar have impoverished themselves by doing so. Economic globalization, in short, may be a necessary, though not sufficient, condition for combating poverty.

The complexities of globalization have led to calls for a global institutional response. Although a hierarchical world government is neither feasible nor desirable, many forms of global governance and methods of managing common affairs already exist and can be expanded. Hundreds of organizations now regulate the global dimensions of trade, telecommunications, civil aviation, health, the environment, meteorology, and many other issues.

Antiglobalization protesters complain that international institutions are illegitimate because they are undemocratic. But the existing global institutions are quite weak and hardly threatening. Even the much-maligned World Trade Organization (WTO) has only a small budget and staff. Moreover, unlike self-appointed nongovernmental organizations (NGOs), international institutions tend to be highly responsive to national governments and can thus claim some real, if indirect, democratic legitimacy. International economic institutions, moreover, merely facilitate cooperation among member states and derive some authority from their efficacy.

Even so, in a world of transnational politics where democracy has become the touchstone of legitimacy, these arguments probably will not be enough to protect any but the most technical organizations from attack. International institutions may be weak, but their rules and resources can have powerful effects. The protesters, moreover, make some valid points. Not all member states of international organizations are themselves democratic. Long lines of delegation from multiple governments, combined with a lack of transparency, often weaken accountability. And although the organizations may be agents of states, they often represent only certain parts of those states. Thus trade ministers attend WTO meetings, finance ministers attend the meetings of the International Monetary Fund (IMF), and central bankers meet at the Bank for International Settlements in Basel. To outsiders, even within the same government, these institutions can look like closed and secretive clubs. Increasing the perceived legitimacy of international governance is therefore an important objective and requires three things: greater clarity about democracy, a richer understanding of accountability, and a willingness to experiment.

We, the People

Democracy requires government by officials who are accountable and removable by the majority of people in a jurisdiction, together with protections for individual and minority rights. But who are "we the people" in a world where political identity at the global level is so weak? "One state, one vote" is not democratic. By that formula, a citizen of the Maldive Islands would have a thousand times more voting power than would a citizen of China. On the other hand, treating the world as a single global constituency in which the majority ruled would mean that the more than 2 billion Chinese and Indians could usually get their way. (Ironically, such a world would be a nightmare for those antiglobalization NGOs that seek international environmental and labor standards, since such measures draw little support from Indian or Chinese officials.)

In a democratic system, minorities acquiesce to the will of the majority when they feel they are generally full-fledged participants in the larger community. There is little evidence, however, that such a strong sense of community exists at the global level today, or that it could soon be created. In its absence, the extension of domestic voting procedures to the global level makes little practical or normative sense. A stronger European Parliament may reduce the "democratic deficit" within a union of relatively homogeneous European states, but it is doubtful that such an institution makes sense for the world at large. Alfred, Lord Tennyson's "Parliament of man" made for great Victorian poetry, but it does not stand up to contemporary political analysis. Democracy, moreover, exists today only in certain well-ordered nation-states, and that condition is likely to change only slowly.

Still, governments can do several things to respond to the concerns about a global democratic deficit. First, they can try to design international institutions that preserve as much space as possible for domestic political processes to operate. In the WTO, for example, the procedures for settling disputes can intrude on domestic sovereignty, but a country can reject a judgment if it pays carefully limited compensation to the trade partners injured by its actions. And if a country does defect from its WTO trade agreements, the settlement procedure limits the kind of tit-for-tat downward spiral of retaliation that so devastated the world economy in the 1930s. In a sense, the procedure is like having a fuse in the electrical system of a house: better the fuse blow than the house burn down. The danger with the WTO, therefore, is not that it prevents member states from accommodating domestic political choices but rather that members will be tempted to litigate too many disputes instead of resolving them through the more flexible route of political negotiations.

Clearer Connections

Better accountability can and should start at home. If people believe that WTO meetings do not adequately account for environmental standards, they can press their governments to include environment ministers or officials in their WTO delegations. Legislatures can hold hearings before or after meetings, and legislators can themselves become national delegates to various organizations.

Governments should also make clear that democratic accountability can be quite indirect. Accountability is often assured through means other than voting, even in well-functioning democracies. In the United States, for example, the Supreme Court and the Federal Reserve Board respond to elections indirectly through a long chain of delegation, and judges and government bankers are kept accountable by professional norms and standards, as well. There is no reason that indirect accountability cannot be consistent with democracy, or that international institutions such as the IMF and the World Bank should be held to a higher standard than are domestic institutions.

Increased transparency is also essential. In addition to voting, people in democracies debate issues using a variety of means, from letters to polls to protests. Interest groups and a free press play important roles in creating transparency in domestic democratic politics and can do so at the international level as well. NGOs are self-selected, not democratically elected, but they too can play a positive role in increasing transparency. They deserve a voice, but not a vote. For them to fill this role, they need information from and dialogue with international institutions. In some instances, such as judicial procedures or market interventions, it is unrealistic to provide information in advance, but records and justifications of decisions can later be disclosed for comment and criticism—as the Federal Reserve and the Supreme Court do in domestic politics. The same standards of transparency should be applied to NGOs themselves, perhaps encouraged by other NGOs such as Transparency International.

The private sector can also contribute to accountability. Private associations and codes, such as those established by the international chemical industry in the aftermath of the Bhopal disaster, can prevent a race to the bottom in standards. The practice of "naming and shaming" has helped consumers hold transnational firms accountable in the toy and apparel industries. And although people have unequal votes in markets, the aftermath of the Asian financial crisis may have led to more increases in transparency by corrupt governments than any formal agreements did. Open markets can help diminish the undemocratic power of local monopolies and reduce the power of entrenched and unresponsive government bureaucracies, particularly in countries where parliaments are weak. Moreover, efforts by investors to increase transparency and legal predictability can spill over to political institutions.

New Democrats

Rather than merely rejecting the poorly formulated arguments of the protesters, proponents of international institutions should experiment with ways to improve accountability. Transparency is essential, and international organizations can provide more access to their deliberations, even if after the fact. NGOs could be welcomed as observers (as the World Bank has done) or allowed to file "friend of the court" briefs in WTO dispute-settlement cases. In some cases, such as the Internet Corporation for Assigned Names and Numbers (which is incorporated as a nonprofit institution under the laws of California), experiments with direct voting for board members may prove fruitful, although the danger of their being taken over by well-organized interest groups remains a problem.

Hybrid network organizations that combine governmental, intergovernmental, and nongovernmental representatives, such as the World Commission on Dams or U.N. Secretary-General Kofi Annan's Global Compact, are other avenues to explore. Assemblies of parliamentarians can also be associated with some organizations to hold hearings and receive information, even if not to vote. In the end, there is no single answer to the question of how to reconcile the necessary global institutions with democratic accountability. Highly technical organizations may be able to derive their legitimacy from their efficacy alone. But the more an institution deals with broad values, the more its democratic legitimacy becomes relevant. People concerned about democracy will need to think harder about norms and procedures for the governance of globalization. Neither denying the problem nor yielding to demagogues in the streets will do.

———■———

As trade barriers fall and markets open, multinational companies can move more easily into countries and purchase government-owned services. This growing push to privatize public water supplies and other basic services in developing countries raises many questions. Proponents say private industry is more efficient than government. Companies can provide better services at a lower cost; they have more technical expertise and capital to invest in improvements. Yet critics say foreign corporations may not care about the best interests of local people. Governments make money in the short run, but people will likely pay more for basic services, and future profits will flow out of the country. Also, foreign companies may not take the long view when making decisions.

*In the case of privatized water supplies, overuse can lead to
critical shortages. Like many developing countries, Bolivia,
a poor nation divided by race and class, is in a bitter struggle
over how much of its natural resources will go into the hands
of foreign investors. —AM*

"Plunder and Profit"
by David Moberg
In These Times, **March 4, 2004**

In September 1999, Bolivian officials signed a 40-year contract
with a private company named Aguas del Tunari to take over
the municipal water system of Cochabamba, the country's third
largest city. The company, largely owned by U.S. construction
giant Bechtel, was the sole bidder for the contract, which
guaranteed 15 percent annual profit in inflation-indexed dollars.

With the encouragement of the International Monetary
Fund (IMF) and the World Bank, since 1985 Bolivian governments have sold national public assets to foreign investors and
opened their markets to global trade. Despite the promise of
development by following the "Washington consensus" of
economic liberalization, it remained the poorest country in Latin
America. But World Bank officials still insisted that Bolivia
privatize Cochabamba's water utility and that residents, no
matter how poor, pay full cost of the service without subsidy.

Two months after Bechtel's subsidiary took over, it
roughly tripled local water rates, telling the poor they could
pay one-fourth of their income for water or have the spigot
shut off. There were massive protests for several months until
the contract was cancelled.

But a few months after signing the contract, Bechtel surreptitiously added new investors and reincorporated its subsidiary in the Netherlands. When it lost the contract, Bechtel sued Bolivia—under terms of a bilateral investment treaty between Bolivia and Netherlands—for damages of at least $25 million for loss of profits it might have made, even though it had invested less than $1 million. Last month, the Bolivian government argued in secret hearings before an investment tribunal affiliated with the World Bank that the treaty doesn't apply, partly because Dutch nationals never controlled Aguas del Tunari.

Cochabamba remains a celebrated battleground in the intensifying worldwide dispute over the privatization of public services, from water and electrical utilities to education, healthcare and pensions. Its ongoing legal struggle reflects the ways in which poor countries often are pressured to privatize a wide range of public assets and services, and then locked into failed policies by international trade agreements.

Free Market Faith

Rich countries—working through international institutions like the World Bank—rarely help poor countries modernize and strengthen public services. But they often push them to privatize and commercialize public services, a move that they themselves would never make. Leading the tide of globalization, international financial institutions are aggressively and undemocratically promoting an ideological agenda of privatization and commercialization.

"The IMF, the World Bank and the World Trade Organization care about dismantling the state," says Nancy

Alexander, director of the Citizens' Network on Essential Services (CNES), a research and advocacy group. "They're faith-based organizations. They don't care who dismantles the state."

International financial institutions claim that such reforms help reduce poverty, but they often simply are promoting the interests of multinational corporations in water, energy, telecommunications and other industries. Multinational corporate investment in privatization peaked in the late '90s, and many firms have since pulled back in response to protests or financial difficulties. So the World Bank, IMF and related institutions are increasingly offering financial aid, subsidies and guarantees to private multinationals to induce them to privatize.

"In the end, it's not an argument about economics. That's not the bottom line," says Doug Hellinger, executive director of the Development Group on Alternative Policies, which is critical of the IMF and World Bank. "It's ideological, but it's also about giving access to companies on terrific terms. It's really about the IMF representing its northern countries and their corporations."

The World Bank theoretically acknowledges a role for the public sector, but in practice it has pushed privatization since the mid-'80s. This year's budget for water privatization, for example, is triple last year's, and over the past decade the portion of the bank's lending for water projects tied to privatization soared. In 2002 it adopted a strategy that emphasized development led by private corporations, and it works closely with the WTO to impose on poor countries the kinds of pro-corporate policies richer countries have the freedom to negotiate.

Indirect Pressure

When countries suffer from financial crises or crippling debt, the IMF and World Bank often insist on privatization of state-owned enterprises, utilities and social services as a condition for financial help. But sometimes, Alexander explains, they push privatization indirectly. For example, they typically require cuts in government budgets, public services and aid to localities. They press for decentralization of public services, dismantling of utilities into smaller units, assessment of market prices for services and elimination of cross-subsidies that may reduce costs for the poor. Financially squeezed by these policies, municipalities may be tempted to privatize the decentralized services. The multinationals then cherry pick the most profitable pieces serving more affluent urban areas, leaving the government responsible for poor and unprofitable rural areas or urban shantytowns.

While some public services in developing countries work well, others are deeply flawed. But as CNES economist Tim Kessler argues, the World Bank acts as if the only alternative is privatization, not improving public services with outside financial and technical aid and with greater citizen account-ability. In any case, privatized utilities need strong public regulation, which is difficult and expensive to do well. Paradoxically, weak and corrupt governments, whose public services could most benefit from reform, are least able to regulate privatized systems. Often they sell public goods on the cheap to cronies and patrons, making privatization really "briberization," says former World Bank chief economist Joseph E. Stiglitz.

Management Matters

Advocates argue that privatization increases efficiency and investment, fosters competition, shrinks deficits and improves services. There are many instances, such as in Chile, where privatized public enterprises increased efficiency and improved service. But in developed countries public utilities generally are as efficient as or better than private.

In developing countries, there also are countless horror stories of price gouging, poor service, meager investment and discrimination against the poor from every continent and in every arena of privatization. For example, Suez, one of two multinationals controlling at least 70 percent of the world's private water contracts, recently lost or abandoned water operations in Argentina, Philippines and Puerto Rico once hailed as model successes. A newly released study by a network of citizens groups that collaborated with the World Bank, "Structural Adjustment: The SAPRI Report," concluded that privatization did not accelerate growth and the form of ownership did not determine efficiency of services as much as management policy.

Despite the failures of privatization, the World Bank and IMF have not shifted their focus to strengthening and democratizing public services. Instead, they are increasing funding to subsidize, to commercially guarantee and to promote privatization (as head of an expert panel on water infrastructure sponsored by the World Bank and multinational water companies). Former IMF managing director Michel Camdessus who recommended last year that there should be more subsidies and guarantees for water privatizers and that the bank should deal more with state and local governments (which typically are less savvy in negotiating with giant multinationals than national governments).

At the WTO, the richer countries want to include more services under the General Agreement on Trade in Services (GATS), potentially opening historically public functions to competition that would benefit multinational service corporations and would indirectly privatize. Once a service is opened under GATS, countries cannot reverse course—for example, make healthcare an exclusively public service—without paying every country that claims it lost a trade opportunity. GATS rules also would severely restrict domestic regulation of service industries.

If the rich countries, along with the World Bank, IMF and WTO, persist in their current privatizing strategies, Cochabamba may turn out to have been an early skirmish in a much wider war.

———◻———

Canadian journalist Naomi Klein stirred up attention with her 1999 book, No Logo: No Space, No Choice, No Jobs, *a revealing look at the global marketing of brands like Starbucks and McDonald's. According to Klein, the multinational companies market lifestyles, instead of products, and expand their brands into every aspect of our lives, from athletic events to school lunch programs. In the process of worldwide brand marketing and the quest for profit, workers have been exploited, jobs lost, and human rights mostly ignored, she asserted. To combat these problems, Klein urged that governments enforce global labor laws and environmental standards.*

In this 2002 article, Klein continues to sound the alarm about economic and cultural globalization. Globalization has raised barriers rather than taken them down, especially in the developing world, she writes. Privatization, deregulation, and antiunion drives have deprived low-wage workers of freedom and opportunity. In the case of Africa, writes Klein, a whole continent has been left "off the map." —AM

"Don't Fence Us In"
by Naomi Klein
Guardian, October 6, 2002

A few months ago, while riffling through my clippings searching for a lost statistic, I noticed a recurring theme: the fence. The image came up again and again: barriers separating people from previously public resources, locking them away from much needed land and water, restricting their ability to move across borders, to express political dissent, to demonstrate on public streets, even keeping politicians from enacting policies that make sense for the people who elected them. Some of these fences are hard to see, but they exist all the same. A virtual fence goes up around schools in Zambia when an education "user fee" is introduced on the advice of the World Bank, putting classes out of the reach of millions of people. A fence goes up around the family farm in Canada when government policies turn small-scale agriculture into a luxury item, unaffordable in a landscape of tumbling commodity prices and factory farms. There is a real if invisible fence that goes up around clean water in Soweto when prices skyrocket owing to privatization, and residents are forced to turn to contaminated sources. And there is a fence that goes up around the very idea of democracy when Argentina is told it won't get an International Monetary Fund loan unless it further reduces social spending, privatizes more resources and eliminates support to local industries, all in the midst of an economic crisis deepened by those very policies. These fences, of course, are as old as colonialism. "Such usurious operations put bars around free nations," Eduardo Galeano wrote in *Open Veins of Latin America*. He was referring to the terms of a British loan to Argentina in 1824.

Fences have always been a part of capitalism, the only way to protect property from would-be bandits, but the double standards propping up these fences have, of late, become increasingly blatant. Expropriation of corporate holdings may be the greatest sin any socialist government can commit in the eyes of the international financial markets (just ask Venezuela's Hugo Chavez or Cuba's Fidel Castro). But the asset protection guaranteed to companies under free trade deals did not extend to the Argentine citizens who deposited their life savings in Citibank, Scotiabank and HSBC accounts and now find that most of their money has simply disappeared. Neither did the market's reverence for private wealth embrace the US employees of Enron, who found that they had been "locked out" of their privatized retirement portfolios, unable to sell even as Enron executives were frantically cashing in their own stocks.

Meanwhile, some very necessary fences are under attack: in the rush to privatization, the barriers that once existed between many public and private spaces—keeping advertisements out of schools, for instance, profit-making interests out of healthcare, or news outlets from acting purely as promotional vehicles for their owners' other holdings—have nearly all been levelled. Every protected public space has been cracked open, only to be re-enclosed by the market.

Another public-interest barrier under serious threat is the one separating genetically modified crops from crops that have not yet been altered. The seed giants have done such a remarkably poor job of preventing their tampered seeds from blowing into neighboring fields, taking root and cross-pollinating that, in many parts of the world, eating GM-free [genetically modified–free] is no longer even an option—the entire food supply has been contaminated. The fences that protect the public interest seem to be fast disappearing, while the ones that restrict our liberties keep multiplying.

When I first noticed that the image of the fence kept coming up in discussion, debates and in my own writing, it seemed significant to me. After all, the past decade of economic integration has been fuelled by promises of barriers coming down, of increased mobility and greater freedom. And yet 13 years after the celebrated collapse of the Berlin Wall, we are surrounded by fences yet again, cut off—from one another, from the earth and from our own ability to imagine that change is possible. The economic process that goes by the benign euphemism "globalization" now reaches into every aspect of life, transforming every activity and natural resource into a measured and owned commodity. As the Hong Kong–based labor researcher Gerard Greenfield points out, the current stage of capitalism is not simply about trade in the traditional sense of selling more products across borders. It is also about feeding the market's insatiable need for growth by redefining as "products" entire sectors that were previously considered part of "the commons" and not for sale. The invading of the public by the private has reached into categories such as health and education, of course, but also ideas, genes, seeds, now purchased, patented and fenced off, as well as traditional aboriginal remedies, plants, water and even human stem cells. With copyright now the US's single largest export (more than manufactured goods or arms), international trade law must be understood not only as taking down selective barriers to trade but more accurately as a process that systematically puts up new barriers—around knowledge, technology and newly privatized resources. These Trade Related Intellectual Property Rights are what prevent farmers from replanting their Monsanto patented seeds and make it illegal for poor countries to manufacture cheaper generic drugs to get to their needy populations.

Globalization is now on trial because on the other side of all these virtual fences are real people, shut out of schools, hospitals, workplaces, their own farms, homes and communities. Mass privatization and deregulation have bred armies of locked-out people, whose services are no longer needed, whose lifestyles are written off as "backward," whose basic needs go unmet. These fences of social exclusion can discard an entire industry, and they can also write off an entire country, as has happened to Argentina. In the case of Africa, essentially an entire continent can find itself exiled to the global shadow world, off the map and off the news, appearing only during wartime when its citizens are looked on with suspicion as potential militia members, would-be terrorists or anti-American fanatics.

In fact, remarkably few of globalization's fenced-out people turn to violence. Most simply move: from countryside to city, from country to country. And that's when they come face to face with distinctly unvirtual fences, the ones made of chain link and razor wire, reinforced with concrete and guarded with machine guns. Whenever I hear the phrase "free trade," I can't help picturing the caged factories I visited in the Philippines and Indonesia that are all surrounded by gates, watchtowers and soldiers—to keep the highly subsidized products from leaking out and the union organizers from getting in. I think, too, about a recent trip to the South Australian desert where I visited the infamous Woomera detention center. At Woomera, hundreds of Afghan and Iraqi refugees, fleeing oppression and dictatorship in their own countries, are so desperate for the world to see what is going on behind the fence that they stage hunger strikes, jump off the roofs of their barracks, drink shampoo and sew their mouths shut.

These days, newspapers are filled with gruesome accounts of asylum seekers attempting to make it across national borders by hiding themselves among the products that enjoy so much more mobility than they do. In December 2001, the bodies of eight Romanian refugees, including two children, were discovered in a cargo container filled with office furniture; they had asphyxiated during the long journey at sea. The same year, the bodies of two more refugees were discovered in Eau Claire, Wisconsin, in a shipment of bathroom fixtures. The year before, 58 Chinese refugees suffocated in the back of a delivery truck in Dover [Britain].

All these fences are connected: the real ones, made of steel and razor wire, are needed to enforce the virtual ones, the ones that put resources and wealth out of the hands of so many. It simply isn't possible to lock away this much of our collective wealth without an accompanying strategy to control popular unrest and mobility. Security firms do their biggest business in the cities, where the gap between rich and poor is greatest—Johannesburg, São Paulo, New Delhi—selling iron gates, armored cars, elaborate alarm systems and renting out armies of private guards. Brazilians, for instance, spend US$4.5 [billion] a year on private security, and the country's 400,000 armed rent-a-cops outnumber actual police officers by almost four to one. In deeply divided South Africa, annual spending on private security has reached US$1.6 [billion], more than three times what the government spends each year on affordable housing. It now seems that these gated compounds protecting the haves from the have-nots are microcosms of what is fast becoming a global security state—not a global village intent on lowering walls and barriers, as we were promised, but a network of fortresses connected by highly militarized trade corridors.

If this picture seems extreme, it may only be because most of us in the west rarely see the fences and the artillery. The gated factories and refugee detention centers remain tucked away in remote places, less able to pose a direct challenge to the seductive rhetoric of the borderless world. But over the past few years, some fences have intruded into full view—often, fittingly, during the summits where this brutal model of globalization is advanced. It is now taken for granted that if world leaders want to get together to discuss a new trade deal, they will need to build a modern-day fortress to protect themselves from public rage. When

Quebec City hosted the Summit of the Americas in April 2001, the Canadian government took the unprecedented step of building a cage around not just the conference center, but the downtown core, forcing residents to show official documentation to get to their homes and workplaces. Another popular strategy is to hold the summits in inaccessible locations: the 2002 G8 meeting was held deep in the Canadian Rocky Mountains, and the 2001 WTO meeting took place in the repressive Gulf State of Qatar, where the emir bans political protests. The "war on terrorism" has become yet another fence to hide behind, used by summit organizers to explain why public shows of dissent just won't be possible this time around or, worse, to draw threatening parallels between legitimate protesters and terrorists bent on destruction.

But what are reported as menacing confrontations are often joyous events, as much experiments in alternative ways of organizing societies as criticisms of existing models. The first time I participated in one of these counter-summits, I remember having the distinct feeling that some sort of political portal was opening up—a gateway, a window, "a crack in history," to use subcomandante Marcos's beautiful phrase. This opening had little to do with the broken window at the local McDonald's, the image so favored by TV cameras; it was something else: a sense of possibility, a blast of fresh air, oxygen rushing to the brain. These protests—which are actually week-long marathons of intense education on global politics, late-night strategy sessions in six-way simultaneous translation, festivals of music and street theater—are like stepping into a parallel universe. Overnight, the site is transformed into a kind of alternative global city, where urgency replaces resignation, corporate logos need armed guards, people usurp cars, art is everywhere, strangers talk to each other, and the prospect of a radical change in political course does not seem like an odd and anachronistic idea but the most logical thought in the world. Even the heavy-handed security measures have been co-opted by activists into part of the message: the fences that surround the summits become metaphors for an economic model that exiles billions to poverty and exclusion. Confrontations are staged at the fence—but not only the ones involving sticks and bricks: tear-gas canisters have been flicked back with hockey sticks, water cannons have been irreverently challenged with toy water pistols and buzzing helicopters mocked with swarms of paper aeroplanes. During the Summit of the Americas in Quebec City, a group of activists built a medieval-style wooden catapult, wheeled it up to the 3m-high fence that enclosed the downtown and lofted teddy bears over the top. In Prague, during a meeting of the World Bank and the International Monetary Fund, the Italian direct-action group Tute Bianche decided not to confront the black-clad riot police dressed in similarly threatening ski masks and bandanas; instead, they marched to the police line in white jumpsuits stuffed with rubber tires and Styrofoam padding. In a standoff between Darth Vader and an army of Michelin Men, the police couldn't win. These activists are quite serious in their desire to disrupt the current economic order, but their tactics reflect a dogged refusal to engage in classic power struggles: their goal is not to take power for themselves but to challenge power centralization on principle.

Other kinds of windows are opening as well, quiet conspiracies to reclaim privatized spaces and assets for public use. Maybe it's students kicking ads out of their classrooms, or swapping music online, or setting up independent media centres with free software. Maybe it's Thai peasants planting organic vegetables on over-irrigated golf courses, or landless farmers in Brazil cutting down fences around unused lands and turning them into farming cooperatives. Maybe it's Bolivian workers reversing the privatisation of their water supply, or South African township residents reconnecting their neighbors' electricity under the slogan Power to the People. And once reclaimed, these spaces are also being remade. In neighborhood assemblies, at city councils, in independent media centers, in community-run forests and farms, a new culture of vibrant direct democracy is emerging, one that is fuelled and strengthened by direct participation, not dampened and discouraged by passive spectatorship.

Despite all the attempts at privatization, it turns out that there are some things that don't want to be owned. Music, water, seeds, electricity, ideas—they keep bursting out of the confines erected around them. They have a natural resistance to enclosure, a tendency to escape, to cross-pollinate, to flow through fences and flee out open windows.

It is not clear what will emerge from these liberated spaces, or if what emerges will be hardy enough to withstand the mounting attacks from the police and military, as the line between terrorist and activist is deliberately blurred. The question of what comes next preoccupies me, as it does everyone else who has been part of building this international movement. As I look again at these article clippings, I see them for what they are: postcards from dramatic moments in time, a record of the first chapter in a very old and recurring story, the one about people pushing up against the barriers that try to contain them, opening up windows, breathing deeply, tasting freedom.

CHAPTER THREE

SCIENCE, TECHNOLOGY, AND SOCIETY: HOW THE WORLD'S INCREASING TECHNOLOGY HAS PAVED THE WAY FOR GLOBALIZATION

The Internet has been a critical factor in the enormous reach of globalization. Conceived in the 1960s as a way to connect university and government research centers, the Internet and the World Wide Web are now accessible to nearly 12 percent of the world's population. In 2003, close to 676 million people had access to the Internet, with 36 percent of those people in developing countries, according to the United Nations's E-Commerce and Development Report 2004. As of June 2004, billions of Web sites were running. With a click of the mouse, a New Yorker can read a South African newspaper; buy pottery from Spain; play an online video game with a South Korean; trade stocks; or write an e-mail to a colleague in Paris.

Bill Gates, chairman and chief software architect at Microsoft, has been at the forefront of this technological revolution. In the following speech, he describes the challenges facing us in a world that is online. —AM

From "Shaping the Internet Age"
by Bill Gates
Internet Policy Institute, December 2000

Less than a quarter of a century ago, the Internet was an obscure network of large computers used only by a small community of researchers. At the time, the majority of computers were found in corporate information technology (IT) departments or research laboratories, and hardly anyone imagined that the Internet would play such an important role in our lives as it does today. In fact, the very idea of a "personal computer," much less millions of them connected by a global network, seemed absurd to all but a handful of enthusiasts.

Today, the Internet is far from obscure—it's the center of attention for businesses, governments and individuals around the world. It has spawned entirely new industries, transformed existing ones, and become a global cultural phenomenon. But despite its impact, today's Internet is still roughly where the automobile was during the era of Henry Ford's Model T. We've seen a lot of amazing things so far, but there is much more to come. We are only at the dawn of the Internet Age.

In the years ahead, the Internet will have an even more profound effect on the way we work, live and learn. By enabling instantaneous and seamless communication and commerce around the globe, from almost any device imaginable, this technology will be one of the key cultural and economic forces of the early 21st century.

Why is the Internet such a powerful and compelling technology? First and foremost, from its conception in the academic community (largely as a result of government-sponsored research) to its subsequent development and commercialization by the private sector, the Internet has evolved into a uniquely independent information exchange—one that is able to grow organically, can operate reliably with little centralized management, and is built entirely on common standards.

It is those common standards that helped make the Internet so successful. From TCP/IP (the technological protocol that is the "traffic cop" for Internet data) to HTML and XML (the twin lingua francas of the World Wide Web), common standards have opened up the Internet to anyone who speaks its language. And since the language of the Internet is universal and easily grasped, any business can create products and services that make use of it. That openness has produced amazing technological competitiveness. To thrive on the Internet, every business has to make its products, services and interface more attractive than competitors that are only a few mouse-clicks away.

The "killer application" that transformed the Internet into a global phenomenon was the World Wide Web. Developed in the late 1980s at the European Center for Nuclear Research (CERN) from research by Tim Berners-Lee, the Web was initially created to share data on nuclear physics. By using hyperlinks and graphical "browsing" technology, the Web greatly simplifies the process of searching for, accessing, and sharing information on the Internet, making it much more accessible to a non-technical audience.

As the Web's popularity surged among students, researchers and other Internet enthusiasts, an entirely new industry emerged to create software and content for the Web.

This explosion of creativity made the Web more compelling for users, which encouraged more companies to provide Internet access, which encouraged still more individuals and businesses to get connected to the Internet. As recently as 1994, there were only 500 fairly modest Web sites worldwide; today the Web has close to 3 billion pages. We can expect this growth cycle to continue and even accelerate, thanks to more powerful and cheaper computers, higher-speed Internet access on a wider range of devices, and advanced software that makes it all work together.

Breaking Down Barriers

The main advantage of any new technology is that it amplifies human potential. In the 20th century, electricity, the telephone, the automobile and the airplane all made the world more accessible to more people, transforming our economy and society in the process. The Internet has the same revolutionary impact—individuals and businesses can overcome geographical, cultural and logistical barriers and improve the way they live and work. Because it amplifies our potential in so many ways, it's possible that the long-term impact of the Internet could equal that of electricity, the automobile and the telephone all rolled together. How?

The Internet makes the world smaller. The ability to communicate and exchange information instantaneously and across vast distances has enabled more individuals and businesses to participate in the economy, regardless of their location. Large companies can connect with employees, suppliers, and partners around the globe, and small businesses can find their customers anywhere in the world. Businesses can hire knowledge workers almost regardless of where they are, greatly expanding employment opportunities for people in the United States, and giving developing nations the ability to become economic powerhouses by providing information technology services to the rest of the world. The Internet, along with other computer technologies, is literally enabling some developing countries to "leapfrog" the industrial revolution and jump straight to the Internet Age.

The Internet brings people closer together. Before the Internet, it was possible to keep in touch with relatives and friends across the country or around the world—but it was also expensive. Today, communicating with a friend in Japan is as easy and cheap as communicating with a friend across town, and families regularly use the Internet to keep in touch with far-flung relatives. Millions of people with shared interests—no matter how obscure—exchange information and build communities through Web sites, email and instant-messaging software. Using innovative accessibility aids, people with disabilities can use the Internet to help overcome barriers that prevent them from leading more productive and fulfilling lives.

The Internet makes the world simpler. For businesses, the Internet breaks down logistical barriers, offering greater flexibility and power in the way they do business. It shrinks time and distance, simplifies complex business processes, and enables more effective communication and collaboration— a giant corporation can now be as nimble as a tiny startup, while a family firm located in a remote rural village now has the world as its marketplace. Combined with advanced productivity software, the Internet enables individual knowledge workers to use their time more efficiently, and to focus on more productive tasks. And it gives consumers the ability to shop smarter, to find the best products at the right prices. In fact, it empowers them in ways that once were available only to large companies, enabling them to join with others to buy products at lower prices, and bid competitively around the world.

What's Next?

The Internet has already revolutionized the way we live and work, but it is still in its infancy. In the coming years, a combination of cheap and powerful computing devices, fast and convenient Internet access, and software innovations could make the Internet as common and powerful a resource as electricity is today.

Today, most people access the Internet through their home or office PC, but as microprocessors become cheaper and more powerful, Internet access will also be available from a wider range of smart devices, from tablet-sized PCs to smart cellular phones—even familiar household appliances. People will be able to share information seamlessly across devices and interact with them in a more natural way, using speech, handwriting and gestures. Eventually, they will be able to interact with a computer almost as easily as they do with each other.

And all this computing power will be interconnected, as high-speed Internet access becomes available in more areas and in many different ways, both wired and wireless. Advances in communications technologies, along with increasing public demand for Internet access, will eventually ensure that Internet connectivity will be commonplace at home, at work or on the move.

Communication between devices on the Internet will be greatly enhanced by new Internet standards such as XML, which offers a way to separate a Web page's underlying data from the presentational view of that data. Whereas HTML uses "tags" to define how data is displayed on Web pages, XML uses tags to provide a common way of defining precisely what the underlying data actually is. XML "unlocks" data so that it can be organized, programmed and edited. This makes it easier for that data to be shared across a wider range of PCs, servers, handheld devices, and "smart" phones and appliances. While today's Internet consists of isolated "islands" of data that are difficult to edit, share and integrate, tomorrow's Internet will break down those barriers and enable people to access and share the information they need—regardless of whether they're accessing the Internet from their PC or any other device.

All these advances will soon create a ubiquitous Internet—personal and business information, email, and instant messaging, rich digital media and Web content will be available any time, any place and from any device.

Opportunities and Challenges

Whenever a new technology emerges with the potential to change the way people live and work, it sparks lively debate about its impact on our world and concern over how widely it should be adopted. Some people will view the technology with tremendous optimism, while others will view it as threatening and disruptive. When the telephone was first introduced, many critics thought it would disrupt society, dissolve communities, erode privacy, and encourage selfish, destructive behavior.

Others thought the telephone was a liberating and democratizing force that would create new business opportunities and bring society closer together.

The Internet brings many of these arguments back to life. Some optimists view the Internet as humanity's greatest invention—an invention on the scale of the printing press. They believe the Internet will bring about unprecedented economic and political empowerment, richer communication between people, a cultural renaissance, and a new era of economic prosperity and world peace. At the other extreme, pessimists think the Internet will result in economic and cultural exploitation, the death of privacy, and a decline in values and social standards.

If history is any guide, neither side of these arguments will be proved right. Just as the telephone, electricity, the automobile, and the airplane shaped our world in the 20th century, the Internet will shape the early years of the 21st, and it will have a profound—and overwhelmingly positive—impact on the way we work and live. But it will not change the fundamental aspects of business and society—companies will still need to make a profit, people will still need their social framework, education will still require great teachers . . .

In his travels as the New York Times *foreign affairs columnist, Thomas L. Friedman has interviewed many people whose lives have changed with the global integration of finance, technology, culture, and politics. In his 1999 best-selling book,* The Lexus and the Olive Tree: Understanding Globalization, *Friedman examines the clash between globalization, local traditions, and*

identity. For Friedman, the Lexus luxury car represents the drive for material wealth, while the olive tree symbolizes the desire to hold on to ancient traditions, family, and cultural identity. He believes the tension between these forces is at the heart of the globalization conflict. Friedman asserts that people and nations may have to give up some of their independence and sovereignty to join the global economy and gain prosperity. He calls these restrictions "golden straitjackets." Still, Friedman's view that globalization is essentially a positive phenomenon, and worth the sacrifices, remains controversial. —AM

From *The Lexus and the Olive Tree: Understanding Globalization*
by Thomas L. Friedman
1999

. . . I was in Tokyo on a reporting assignment and had arranged to visit the Lexus luxury car factory outside Toyota City, south of Tokyo. It was one of the most memorable tours I've ever taken. At that time, the factory was producing 300 Lexus sedans each day, made by 66 human beings and 310 robots. From what I could tell, the human beings were there mostly for quality control. Only a few of them were actually screwing in bolts or soldering parts together. The robots were doing all the work. There were even robotic trucks that hauled materials around the floor and could sense when a human was in their path and would "beep, beep, beep" at them to move. I was fascinated watching the robot that applied the rubber seal that held in place the front windshield of each Lexus. The robot arm would neatly paint the hot molten rubber in a perfect rectangle around the window. But what I liked most was that when it finished its application there was always a tiny drop of rubber left hanging from the tip of the robot's finger—like the drop of toothpaste that might be left at the top of the tube after you've squeezed it onto your toothbrush. At the Lexus factory, though, this robot arm would swing around in a wide loop until the tip met a tiny, almost invisible metal wire that would perfectly slice off that last small drop of hot black rubber—leaving almost nothing left over. I kept staring at this process, thinking to myself how much planning, design, and technology it must have taken to get that robot arm to do its job and then swing around each time, at the precise angle, so that this little thumbnail-size wire could snip of the last drop of hot rubber and start clean on the next window. I was impressed.

After touring the factory, I went back to Toyota City and boarded the bullet train for the ride back to Tokyo. The bullet train is aptly named, for it has both the look and feel of a speeding bullet. As I nibbled away on one of those sushi dinner boxes you can buy in any Japanese train station, I was reading that day's *International Herald Tribune*, and a story caught my eye on the top right corner of page 3. It was about the daily State Department briefing. State Department spokeswoman Margaret D. Tutwiler had given a controversial interpretation of a 1948 United Nations resolution, relating to the right of return for Palestinian refugees to Israel. I don't remember all the details, but whatever the interpretation was, it had clearly agitated both the Arabs and the Israelis and sparked a furor in the Middle East, which the story was reporting.

So there I was speeding along at 180 miles an hour on the most modern train in the world, reading this story about the oldest corner of the world. And the thought occurred to me that these Japanese, whose Lexus factory I had just visited and whose train I was riding, were building the greatest luxury car in the world with robots. And over here, on the top of page 3 of the *Herald Tribune*, the people with whom I had lived for so many years in Beirut and Jerusalem, whom I knew so well, were still fighting over who owned which olive tree. It struck me then that the Lexus and the olive tree were actually pretty good symbols of this post–Cold War era: half the world seemed to be emerging from the Cold War intent on building a better Lexus, dedicated to modernizing, streamlining and privatizing their economies in order to thrive in the system of globalization. And half the world—sometimes half the same country, sometimes half the same person—was still caught up in the fight over who owns which olive tree.

Olive trees are important. They represent everything that roots us, anchors us, identifies us and locates us in the world—whether it be belonging to a family, a community, a tribe, a nation, a religion, or, most of all, a place called home. Olive trees are what give us the warmth of family, the joy of individuality, the intimacy of personal rituals, the depth of private relationships, as well as the confidence and security to reach out and encounter others. We fight so intensely at times over our olive trees because, at their best, they provide the feelings of self-esteem and belonging that are as essential for human survival as food in the belly. At worst, though, when taken to excess, an obsession with our olive trees leads us to forge identities, bonds and communities based on the exclusion of others, and at their worst, when these obsessions really run amok, as with the Nazis in Germany or the Serbs in Yugoslavia, they lead to the extermination of others.

Conflicts between Serbs and Muslims, Jews and Palestinians, Armenians and Azeris over who owns which olive tree are so venomous precisely because they are about who will be at home and anchored in a local world and who will not be. Their underlying logic is: I must control this olive tree, because if the other controls it, not only will I be economically and politically under his thumb, but my whole sense of home will be lost. I'll never be able to take my shoes off and relax. Few things are more enraging to people than to have their identity or their sense of home stripped away. They will die for it, kill for it, sing for it, write poetry for it and novelize about it. Because without a sense of home and belonging, life becomes barren and rootless. And life as a tumbleweed is no life at all.

So then what does the Lexus represent? It represents an equally fundamental, age-old human drive—the drive for sustenance, improvement, prosperity and modernization—as it is played out in today's globalization system. The Lexus represents all the burgeoning global markets, financial institutions and computer technologies with which we pursue higher living standards today. Yet, for millions of people in developing countries, the quest for material improvement still involves walking to a well, plowing a field barefoot behind an ox or gathering wood and carrying it on their heads for five miles. These people still upload for a living, not download.

For millions of others in developed countries, though, this quest for material betterment and modernization is increasingly conducted in Nike shoes, shopping in integrated markets and using the new network technologies. While different people

have different access to the new markets and technologies
that characterize the globalization system, and derive highly
unequal benefits from them, this doesn't change the fact that
they are the defining economic tools of the day and everyone
is either directly or indirectly affected by them.

The Lexus versus the olive tree, though, is just a modern
version of a very old story—indeed one of the oldest stories in
recorded history—the story of why Cain slew Abel. The
Hebrew Bible says in Genesis: "Cain said to his brother Abel;
And when they were in the field, Cain rose up against his
brother Abel and killed him. Then the Lord said to Cain,
'Where is your brother Abel?' And he said, 'I do not know.
Am I my brother's keeper?' And the Lord said, 'What have
you done? The voice of your brother's blood is crying to me
from the ground.'"

If you read this paragraph closely you notice that the
Hebrew Bible never tells us what Cain actually said to Abel.
The sentence reads that "Cain said to his brother Abel," and
then it just stops. We are not privy to the conversation. What
happened in the conversation between them that got Cain so
angry that he would actually kill his brother Abel? My theology
teacher, Rabbi Tzvi Marx, taught me that the rabbinic sages in
Genesis Rabbah, one of the fundamental rabbinic commentaries
on the Bible, give three basic explanations of what was said.
One is that the two brothers were arguing about a woman—
Eve. After all, there was only one women on Earth at the time,
their mother, and they were arguing over which brother would
get to marry her. They were arguing over sexual fulfillment
and procreation. Another interpretation posits that Cain and
Abel had basically divided up the world between them. Cain had

all the real estate—or as the Bible says, "Cain became tiller of the soil"—and Abel had all the movables and livestock—"Abel became a keeper of the sheep." And according to this interpretation, Cain told Abel to get his sheep off Cain's property and this triggered a fight over territory that eventually ended with Cain slaying Abel in the heat of the argument. They were fighting over economic development and mutual fulfillment. The third interpretation is that the two brothers had neatly divided everything in the world between them, except one critical thing that was still up for grabs: Where would the Temple be built that would reflect their particular religious and cultural identity? Each wanted to control that Temple and have it reflect his identity. Each wanted that Temple in his olive grove. They were fighting over the issue of identity, and which of them would be the keeper of their family's source of legitimacy. So, the rabbis noted, all the basic elements of human motivation are potentially there in one story: the need for sexual intimacy, the need for sustenance and the need for a sense of identity and community. I will leave matters of sex for someone else. This book is about the other two.

That's why I like to say that information arbitrage provides the lenses we need to look into today's world, but lenses alone are not enough. We also need to know what we are looking at and for. And what we are looking at and for is how the age-old quests for material betterment and for individual and communal identity—which go all the way back to Genesis—play themselves out in today's dominant international system of globalization. This is the drama of the Lexus and the olive tree.

In 1944, the leaders of the Allied nations met at Bretton Woods, New Hampshire, and created the World Bank and the International Monetary Fund, which were fully established in 1946. World War II had destroyed much of Europe, and the bank's purpose was to help rebuild. In 1947, the bank made its first loan, providing $250 million to France for postwar reconstruction. The bank soon changed its focus to reducing world poverty through loans to developing countries. Chile received the bank's first development loans for hydroelectric projects in 1948.

Today, the World Bank Group, with 184 member nations, comprises five development institutions that provide loans and technical advice for projects such as educating girls in Bangladesh, improving health care in Mexico, and fighting AIDS in Guinea. In 2004, the World Bank gave $20.1 billion for 245 projects. Still, the bank has been criticized for not always ensuring that the money goes directly to the people it's supposed to help.

In this essay, World Bank president James D. Wolfensohn (1995–2005) says that fighting world poverty will take global cooperation. —AM

"A Call to Global Action"
by James D. Wolfensohn
America, January 8, 2001

The new millennium, with all its promise of change, presents us with a profound challenge: how to stem the rising incidence of global poverty. It is surely a major piece of unfinished business carried over from the previous century—how to give the poorest people of the world real hope for a better life.

The urgency of this task cannot be disputed. While recent decades have seen major improvements in the health and education of many people, reflected in falling infant mortality rates, rising life expectancy and increasing literacy rates, three billion other people, half the world's population, live on less than $2 a day. By 2025, that figure may rise to four billion. As many as 110 million children, most of them girls, do not attend primary school. More than 30 million people live with H.I.V.-AIDS.

It is clear that unless we in the worldwide community can show more tangible results in the battle against hunger and deprivation, against the continuing human devastation caused by communicable diseases, against unsustainable debt for the poorest countries and against the digital divide with its threat of keeping developing countries disconnected from the wealth of the digital revolution, this new millennium of ours, from which we expect so much, will almost certainly produce a more fractured, unequal and turbulent era.

Despite years of relative peace and prosperity in industrialized countries, global poverty is getting worse. More troubling still is the massive and widening gap between rich and poor. There are those who argue that global economic integration is behind these alarming numbers. And to be sure, the benefits of globalization are not evenly spread. This needs to be addressed, but simply blaming globalization does not help.

Over the last century, the forces of globalization have been among those that have contributed to a huge improvement in human welfare, including raising countless millions out of poverty. Going forward, these forces have the potential to continue bringing great benefits to the poor, but how strongly they do so will also continue to depend crucially on factors such as the quality of overall macroeconomic policies, the workings of institutions and social safety nets, among many others.

There is much to be done, therefore, if we are to ensure that all countries, especially the poorest, benefit from this process. We cannot turn back globalization; our challenge is to make it an instrument of opportunity and inclusion, not of fear and insecurity.

To meet this challenge, we at the World Bank have deepened our understanding of what poverty is and how to generate equitable development.

We have learned that poverty is about more than inadequate income or even low human development. Poverty, as discussions with 60,000 poor people in 60 countries have taught us, is multidimensional and complex. It is about lack of fundamental freedom of action, choice and opportunity. It is voicelessness, powerlessness, insecurity and humiliation.

We have also learned that market-oriented reforms, if combined with social and institutional development, can deliver economic growth to poor people. Growth is the most powerful force for sustained poverty reduction. It is crucial, but it is not enough. Experience has shown us that growth leads to larger and quicker reductions in poverty if measures are taken to empower the poor and to enhance their security.

To be successful, development must be comprehensive. It needs to embrace sound economic policies and infrastructure, but also education, health, good governance, the fight against corruption, legal and judicial reform and environmental protection. All these elements depend on and reinforce one another.

Without a comprehensive approach that is crafted and adopted in each country, we will not achieve the development that is vital for a peaceful, equitable world.

To improve our work we are applying what we have learned, and we are changing our institution and the way we do business to deliver more effectively, transparently and with greater accountability. We are working with our colleagues in the United Nations system and the other multilateral development banks on selectivity and the division of labor among us. We are working with governments, helping them to take forward their policies and institutions rather than simply implementing our projects.

Last year we launched the Comprehensive Development Framework—a holistic, long-term and country-owned approach that is being implemented in a dozen countries. With the International Monetary Fund, we began supporting our partner countries in their work on poverty reduction strategies— strategies that are country-driven and focused on poverty. Our comprehensive framework and the poverty reduction strategies embody an approach to poverty reduction that is gaining strong recognition in the development community.

We have increased our lending in social sectors. In 1980, investment in the power sector accounted for 21 percent of bank lending. Today, that figure is down to 2 percent. By contrast, lending for health, nutrition and education has expanded almost fivefold from 5 percent in 1980 to over 22 percent today. The bank is also doing more on social protection—on safety nets in particular—and other key issues like gender.

The World Bank is also working to ease the crippling debt burden the poorest countries face. In 1996, the bank and the I.M.F. launched the Heavily Indebted Poor Countries initiative (H.I.P.C.), the first international response to provide comprehensive debt relief to the world's poorest, most heavily indebted countries. Under the initiative, the debt of more than 30 eligible countries will be cut by $50 billion, with the World Bank reducing its debt claims by nearly $11 billion.

We are also working to stamp out the cancer of corruption, a major inhibitor of development. Corruption in all its forms is a crippling tax on the poor, diverting public services from those who need them most and undermining public support for development aid by creating a false perception that all assistance is affected by corruption.

It is two years since the board of the World Bank endorsed an anticorruption strategy, and the attention given to governance issues inside and outside the bank has increased dramatically. Our dialogue with client countries on these issues has become notably more open, and more than 600 specific anticorruption programs and governance initiatives have been undertaken in almost 100 borrower countries. This is a substantial achievement.

Corruption, by its very nature, will persist as a complex and difficult problem, and the bank and its member countries have to be prepared for a long, hard struggle. In accordance with its role as a development institution working in poor countries that have weak controls and capacities, we can and have helped to bring corruption to the forefront of international attention and are helping to confront the challenge corruption represents. But fighting the cancer of corruption is a challenge not just for the bank, but for the entire development community—international financial institutions and development agencies, civil society, the private and public sectors. If we all move forward with momentum, we have a real chance to make a difference.

As the fight against corruption has shown, most of the issues we face require that we build a concerted coalition of partners ready to supplement national actions with measures at the global level.

Control of communicable disease, for example, is a global public good critical for successful poverty reduction strategies and for development more generally, which requires a major international effort. The bank continues to play a full part in this undertaking—by expanding the scale and flexibility of lending, by tackling disease prevention and control at the source and multisectorally, and by intensifying the engagement with governments to encourage strong nationally driven programs that our lending can then support.

The bank has funded more than 80 H.I.V.-AIDS projects and components around the world totaling nearly $1 billion, and recently made available an additional $500 million in flexible and rapid funding for several projects to fight the epidemic in sub-Saharan African countries.

We acknowledge the fact that high aid dependency can seriously weaken a government's ability to attend to some of the more pressing social needs of its people. Addressing the H.I.V.-AIDS crisis is one of the most urgent concerns of developing countries today. We have a moral obligation to come to the immediate assistance of these countries—not by encouraging countries to borrow to finance H.I.V.-AIDS programs, but by integrating AIDS into debt relief programs. In fact, many of the countries that will benefit from debt relief are countries that are severely affected by the AIDS epidemic.

A second global public good where the bank can make a big impact is in the use of new technology to deliver knowledge where it is needed. Bridging the digital divide is an issue we must all address.

Today we have a unique tool at our disposal to enable involvement of all, on a scale undreamed of just a few years ago. Technology alone will not solve the problems of the developing world, but we believe it can play a major role in helping meet the challenges of poverty. And so, over the last five years, we have been focusing on how we can harness the power of information and communications technology and of knowledge to accelerate development.

The World Bank is working with governments to foster policy, regulatory and network readiness, through our analytical and advisory work and through our grant facility, *info*Dev. We have established direct communications through the African Virtual University, which we created, which is operating in 14 countries, as well as through the partnership for capacity-building in Africa. We have already linked 35,000 school children in 15 developing countries with partner schools in developed countries through our World Links program, providing training and information exchange and joint projects between teachers and students. We have linked the world's leading research institutions with local and regional research institutions in developing countries through the Global Distance Learning Network, providing the possibility of Internet communication and joint research.

The information and communications revolution offers us an unprecedented opportunity to make empowerment and participation a reality. There is no reason why hundreds of millions of people living in Central Asia, Latin America or Africa should be cut off from the ideas that are changing the rest of the world, or why these ideas should not be enriched by their local experience simply because of a lack of readily available cable or satellite technology. The capacity of the Internet—yet to be fully imagined—to eliminate forever the knowledge gap between rich and poor countries may be the single most important determinant of what our world will look like in 50 years.

Education is also key to harnessing knowledge as a major driving force for development. The World Bank will continue to push for a global consensus on the centrality of education for economic and social development and for poverty reduction. We are partnering with others to support countries that are committed to achieving the Education for All goals much sooner than the 2015 timeline and will intensify its efforts to help countries identify priorities and finance and implement national action plans. We will leverage stronger partnerships on core topics such as improving girls' education and providing basic education for the poorest.

The World Bank is committed to working with its partners, including other donors, to ensure that no country with a credible, viable and sustainable education plan will be unable to implement it for lack of external resources.

In assessing which direction to take in the new millennium and how we will harness the forces of globalization to ensure that the opportunities it creates are shared by all, everyone should have a voice, most importantly the poor themselves.

Our challenge is to move beyond the rhetoric and recognize that we live in a time of astonishing possibility. Whether it be immunizing all children against preventable disease or linking every school in Central Asia to the Internet, solutions to problems that seemed insurmountable just a few years ago are now within reach. But in order to provide real solutions to our seemingly intractable problems of poverty and disease, we need to enlist the help of everyone. We must work together to harness the benefits of globalization to deliver prosperity to the many, not just the few.

———■———

The environmental impact of trade expansion and industrialization in developing nations is a critical issue in the globalization debate. Without adequate laws protecting against hazardous waste disposal, air pollution, and clearcutting forests, these countries may face environmental catastrophes, even while their economies grow.

Since the mid-1990s, the World Trade Organization has recognized the tenuous balance between increased trade and a sustainable environment. The added cost of environmentally friendly practices is a stumbling block to action, and some countries and companies may be unwilling or unable to pay the price. Multilateral environment agreements such as the Kyoto Protocol, which mandates industrialized nations to reduce emissions of greenhouse gases, are a step forward, but gaining a consensus is never easy. Maintaining that it could harm the U.S. economy, the Bush administration has refused to ratify the Kyoto agreement.

In this article, Wall Street Journal *reporters describe the disastrous global environmental impact of one factory in China. —AM*

"Invisible Export—A Hidden Cost of China's Growth: Mercury Migration"
by Matt Pottinger, Steve Stecklow, and John J. Fialka
Wall Street Journal, December 20, 2004

On a recent hazy morning in eastern China, the Wuhu Shaoda power company revved up its production of electricity, burning a ton and a half of coal per minute to satisfy more than half the demand of Wuhu, an industrial city of two million people. AES Corp., an American energy company, owns 25% of the 250-megawatt facility, which local officials call an "economically advanced enterprise."

The Chinese plant is outfitted with devices that prevent soot from billowing into the sky. But other pollutants, such as nitrogen oxides, sulfur dioxide and a gaseous form of mercury, swirl freely from the smokestacks. Rather than install more sophisticated and costly antipollution equipment, the plant, which is majority owned by state-controlled entities, has chosen to pay an annual fee, which it estimates will be about $500,000 this year. That option meets Chinese standards but wouldn't be allowed in the U.S.

The airborne output of Chinese power plants like Wuhu Shaoda was once considered the price of China's economic growth, and a mostly local problem. But just as China's industrial might is integrating the country into the global economy, its pollution is also becoming a global concern. Among the biggest worries: the impact of China's vast and growing power industry, mostly fueled by coal, on the buildup of mercury in the world's water and food supply.

Scientists long assumed mercury settled into the ground or water soon after it spewed forth as a gas from smokestacks.

But using satellites, airplanes and supercomputers, scientists are now tracking air pollution with unprecedented precision, discovering plumes of soot, ozone, sulfates and mercury that drift eastward across oceans and continents.

Mercury and other pollutants from China's more than 2,000 coal-fired power plants soar high into the atmosphere and around the globe on what has become a transcontinental conveyor belt of bad air. North America and Europe add their own dirty loads to the belt. But Asia, pulsating with the economic rebirth of China and India, is the largest contributor.

"We're all breathing each other's air," says Daniel J. Jacob, a Harvard professor of atmospheric chemistry and one of the chief researchers in a recent multinational study of transcontinental air pollution. He traced a plume of dirty air from Asia to a point over New England, where samples revealed that chemicals in it had come from China.

One reason China's power industry spews out so much pollution is that under the nation's rules, many plants have the option of paying the government annual fees rather than installing antipollution equipment. Moreover, Beijing officials concede they lack the authority to shut down heavily polluting plants. And local inspectors, who don't report to Beijing, are reluctant to crack down on power companies that generate jobs.

In the U.S., the consequences are being detected not just in the air people breathe but in the food they eat. The U.S. Environmental Protection Agency recently reported that a third of the country's lakes and nearly a quarter of its rivers are now so polluted with mercury that children and pregnant women are advised to limit or avoid eating fish caught there. Warnings about mercury, a highly toxic metal used in things ranging from dental fillings to watch batteries, have been issued by 45 states and cover four of the five Great Lakes. Some scientists now say 30% or more of the mercury settling into U.S. ground soil and waterways comes from other countries—in particular, China.

The increasingly global nature of the problem is rendering local solutions inadequate. Officials in some countries are using the presence of pollution from abroad "as an argument to do nothing [at] home," says Klaus Toepfer, executive director of the United Nations Environment Program in Nairobi, Kenya.

Yet global remedies—primarily treaties—are even harder to achieve. The last such initiative, the Kyoto Protocol, aimed at limiting emissions related to global warming, was rejected by the U.S., the largest contributor of such emissions—and doesn't apply to China, the second-largest emitter. The best shot at a treaty for transcontinental pollution, Mr. Toepfer believes, would be to regulate a single pollutant that everyone agrees is hazardous. He recommends starting with mercury.

China is already believed to be the world's largest source of nonnatural emissions of mercury. Jozef Pacyna, director of the Center for Ecological Economics at the Norwegian Institute for Air Research, calculates that China, largely because of its coal combustion, spews 600 tons of mercury into the air each year, accounting for nearly a quarter of the world's nonnatural emissions. And the volume is rising at a time when North American and European mercury pollution is dropping. The U.S. emitted about 120 tons of mercury into the air in 1999 from manmade sources. Chinese power plants currently under construction—the majority fueled by coal—will alone have more than twice the entire electricity-generating capacity of the U.K.

The overwhelming majority of China's power plants are built, owned and operated by Chinese companies. Speaking about the Wuhu Shaoda power plant, Robin Pence, a spokeswoman for AES, says the Arlington, Va., company "is a minority partner in Wuhu. As such, we neither operate nor control the plant." She adds that AES didn't build the plant and that its world-wide policy for plants that it does design and build is to meet emission standards set either by the local country or the World Bank, whichever are more stringent. The Wuhu plant's manager declined to comment.

Natural Sources

EPA scientists estimate that a third of the mercury in the atmosphere gets there naturally. Traces of the silvery liquid in the earth's crust make their way into the sky through volcanic eruptions and evaporation from the earth's surface. It took the industrial age to turn mercury into a public-health concern. Mining, waste incineration and coal combustion emit the metal in the form of an invisible gas. After it rains down and seeps into wetlands, rivers and lakes, microbes convert it into methylmercury, a compound that works its way up the food chain into fish and eventually people.

The dangers of significant methylmercury exposure to the nervous system are well documented, particularly in fetuses and children. Permanent harm to children can range from subtle deficits in memory and attention span to mental retardation. In January, EPA scientists released research indicating that 630,000 U.S. babies born during a 12-month period in 1999–2000 had potentially unsafe levels of mercury in their blood—about twice as many babies as previously estimated.

Adults aren't immune, either. Joel Bouchard, a National Hockey League defenseman who spent the past two seasons with the New York Rangers, says that last December he began suffering dizziness, headaches, insomnia and blurred vision—forcing him to miss around 25 games. "It was, honestly, like I was in the Twilight Zone," he says. A team doctor discovered Mr. Bouchard had abnormally high levels of mercury in his bloodstream. The suspected cause: the tuna and other fish he'd been eating almost daily as part of what he thought was a healthy diet. He says his blood levels have since returned to normal and the symptoms have disappeared.

Few places more starkly illustrate the threat from mercury, and the obstacles to containing it, than China.

In Qingzhen, a town in the poor mountainous province of Guizhou about 800 miles southwest of Wuhu, a 53-year-old female rice grower who goes by the single name of Zhang and thousands of other farmers are surrounded by mercury pollution. Dark smoke surges from the local power plant, staining crops a drab gray. The plant flushes eight million cubic meters, or about 10 million cubic yards, of ash and water each year into an area adjacent to a major drinking-water reservoir. Some fish near the plant have levels of mercury 18 times what the EPA and the Chinese government consider safe, according to the Guizhou Provincial Environmental Science and Research Institute, which recently did a seven-year study of the province's mercury pollution.

The plots of land that Ms. Zhang and her neighbors tend are especially poorly situated. Nearby is the Guizhou Crystal Organic Chemical factory, which over the years released up to 100 tons of mercury into a stream that runs through her village, according to the study. An official in the factory's environment and safety department calls the report's estimate "too high," and says the factory stopped dumping mercury by 1998. But the stream still runs black and reeks so strongly of chemicals that people unaccustomed to the smell struggle not to gag when standing downwind.

Ms. Zhang and her neighbors are used to the smell. With no other choice, they pump water from the poisoned stream onto dozens of acres of rice paddies each planting season. Rice from the fields tastes sour, she says. "When you wash it, the water in the pot turns the same color as the river." Grain from these fields contains nearly 40 times as much mercury as rice from Shanghai, according to the study. Laboratory mice fed the rice became hyperactive and their nervous systems began deteriorating within a month, the study says.

Farmers in the village complain of periodic fits of shaking. Ms. Zhang suspects the pollution is the reason she and some neighbors have stomach cancer.

Once airborne, by drifting as an invisible gas or clinging to particles of dust, mercury begins to wander. Last April, an instrument-laden U.S. surveillance aircraft near the California-Oregon border hit a plume of dirty air inbound from China. Among the pollutants: black carbon, sulfur dioxide and mercury. "Storms didn't wash it away," marvels Veerabhadran Ramanathan of the Scripps Institution of Oceanography in La Jolla, Calif.

Dr. Ramanathan, who helped pioneer the field of tracking international air pollution, says such plumes shed some of the noxious load over the ocean. But their bulk continues to drift across the U.S. at the leisurely speed of a blimp, polluting lakes and rivers as it goes.

The density of Chinese pollution has amazed researchers. Hans Friedli, a chemist at the National Center for Atmospheric Research in Boulder, Colo., recalls flying through plumes off the Chinese coast near Shanghai two years ago that contained pollutants in the "highest concentration that I have ever seen from an aircraft, except when I've flown into forest fires."

And it is going to get worse. By 2020, China will have nearly 1,000 gigawatts of total electricity-generating capacity, more than twice the current amount, according to the State Power Economic Research Center. The majority of new plants will burn coal. Coal-fired plants today produce three-quarters of the country's electricity, compared with around 50% in the U.S. China will this year burn about 1.9 billion tons of coal, a 12% increase from last year, and consumption is expected to keep rising.

China is phasing in several measures to tackle air pollution. But soot plus sulfur dioxide and nitrogen oxides—often referred to as "SOx and NOx"—are understandably taking priority over mercury. Even with the existence of poisoned villages like Ms. Zhang's, other pollutants affect even more Chinese people. Airborne particulates are a suspected leading cause of respiratory disease around the country. Acid rain from sulfur dioxide now pelts a third of China's territory, a ratio that is "expanding, not shrinking," says Pan Yue, the deputy director of China's State Environmental Protection Administration, or SEPA.

Mr. Pan, an outspoken champion of stricter environmental standards, says there currently aren't any rules being drafted to address mercury. Asked if he is aware of recent studies linking Chinese emissions to mercury in American lakes and rivers, he nods.

"As for China's impact on surrounding countries, I'm first to admit the problem. But let's talk about this in the context of international fairness," he says, before firing rhetorical questions aimed at Washington: "Whose development model are we emulating? Who has been shifting all of its pollution-heavy factories to China? . . . And who bears an even greater international responsibility than China—but has yet to shoulder it—on matters like greenhouse-gas emissions?"

Environmentalists say U.S. action to control its own mercury emissions from power plants has been sluggish. James Connaughton, head of the White House Council on Environmental Quality, counters that the Bush administration has promised by next March to announce regulations aimed specifically at restricting mercury emissions from coal plants, which he calls a "world first." The plan, which follows years of delays and lawsuits, is expected to include market-based trading of pollution credits among utilities and won't be implemented fully until 2018. Other technologies, such as flue gas desulfurisation, that remove some mercury while scrubbing other pollutants from coal have helped cut mercury emissions in Europe and North America.

Weak Incentive

On the face of it, China's new rules on sulfur dioxide should help combat emissions of mercury, too. Beijing is requiring many power plants approved after 1995 to install equipment that reduces sulfur dioxide, and such equipment often has a bonus effect of filtering out some mercury. China this summer also increased the fees that power plants must pay for each ton of sulfur dioxide they emit, hoping the change will give all coal-fired power plants an incentive to buy such equipment.

But the reality is that sheer increases in Chinese coal consumption, together with difficulty policing polluters, will more than offset whatever reductions in sulfur dioxide and mercury are achieved by the rules, experts say. For China, the economics of coal remain irresistible.

It's cheaper, and "with current global reserves, it probably wouldn't be a stretch to keep using coal another 200 years," says Fan Weitang, president of the China National Coal Association. Sitting in his Beijing headquarters at Coal Tower, a sleek new 22-story building, Mr. Fan is caught off guard by questions about mercury pollution. "It is hard for me to discuss that in depth," he says. Other pollutants like airborne particulates, and SO_x and NO_x, receive more attention, and "won't be much of a problem" in the near future, he promises.

That view isn't shared by Chinese scientists. "'No problem'? Big problem," says Tang Dagang, head of atmospheric research at the Academy of Environmental Sciences, which is funded in part by SEPA. By the end of last year, only 5% of the installed capacity of coal-fired plants in China had technology to reduce sulfur dioxide, according to official statistics. While new rules will require the retrofitting of many plants with such technology, Mr. Tang says older plants that account for half of existing power-making capacity are exempt.

What's more, there is little economic incentive for power plants like Wuhu Shaoda, the company partly owned by AES, to further clean up its act.

Next year, Wuhu Shaoda will pay an estimated fee of $400,000 for the several thousand tons it is expected to emit of sulfur dioxide alone, according to an official with knowledge of the plant's emissions. That's much less than the $14.5 million engineers at the plant say it would cost to buy sulfur-dioxide-removal equipment.

CHAPTER FOUR

INDIVIDUAL DEVELOPMENT AND IDENTITY: HOW GLOBALIZATION HAS CHANGED PEOPLES' LIVES

The global job shift has sent many American jobs overseas, mostly to developing countries where labor costs are lower. A great number of the American jobs have gone to India, a country with a skilled, well-educated, and English-speaking workforce. Some of the jobs are upscale and pay well, such as positions in radiology, publishing, and computer programming. Others provide a temporary paycheck but little security. An example of this type of job is in the telemarketing industry. Most Americans have received telemarketing calls from India in the past several years for everything from mortgages to phone services.

In this article, Indian writers Nidhi Kumar and Nidhi Verghese explore what it's like to work at a call center in India. They question whether telemarketing jobs offer real opportunities to young Indians. Instead, they suggest, it is the multinational company that is the chief beneficiary of a cheap and willing labor force—and the shift of jobs overseas is not really improving the lives of the workers in India and other developing countries. —AM

"Money for Nothing and the Calls for Free"

by Nidhi Kumar and Nidhi Verghese
CorpWatch.org, February 17, 2004

The teacher lights a candle. The student whispers a thank you, gently blowing out the candle. The candle is relit. Once again the student says thank you the flame flickers and then glows steadily. The teacher smiles. Another day, another lesson learnt.

This is one of the exercises in an accent neutralization class in India. Many such training institutes have sprung up which prepare youngsters for working in call centers. Call centers are mushrooming around the country and youngsters are queuing up to join the "may I help you" brigade.

The Customer Service Executives (CSEs), or agents, keep in touch with foreign clients, sell products to prospective customers, offer after-sales services, handle queries, attend to complaints, etc. The CSEs assume different names and identities. They are trained to understand and speak with a neutral accent.

Growth Industry

Call centers provide employment on a large scale in India; currently, about 200,000 young men and women are working in call centers. They are mostly restricted to metropolitan cities and recruit youngsters from the upper middle class bracket.

According to a research done by callcentre.net, an Australian research and consulting firm, the Indian call center industry is expected to grow by 68 percent in the next twelve months, overtaking Australia to become the largest call center country across Asia by 2004. If one starts out as an agent in a call center, one can become the manager in just a few years. An entry-level worker earns about 100,000 rupees ($2,211) a year.

According to call center representatives, the pace at which wages are raised is exceptionally fast. An official from a call center recruitment and training center in Mumbai says, "There is room for both horizontal and vertical development. In five years one can go from a CSE to an Operations Manager, earning 50,000 rupees ($1,105) a month."

Elsy Thomas, Head of Economics Department, Sophia College, has a different point of view. She says, "Growth may be fast but what does one do after five years? There is stagnation and there is no new learning. However, Call centers have proved beneficial to India."

According to US State Legislation, all products that cost more than one dollar require customer service operations that are often relocated to developing countries like India. There is much hype about how India could become the global hub for outsourced businesses.

But the reality is that the current boom is based on a single premise—cheap labor. But is cheap labor a virtue? Is it something to be proud of? The call center industry could move overnight to another country where the cost of labor would be lower. In the US, a CSE is paid eight dollars per hour whereas in India they are paid 72 cents for the same work.

Physical Costs

The job comes with all sorts of problems. The working hours at call centers are odd, due to the time difference in various countries. Centers offer pick-up and drop-back facilities but only at night. Sameer used to work at Wipro Spectramind at Powai, Mumbai during the graveyard shift from 2:30 AM to 10:00 AM. "Traveling by locals, at rush hour, after a sleepless night's work was extremely tiring," he says. Besides the odd working hours, repeating the same task over and over again can be very monotonous.

Mayur, who recently quit his job at Epicenter in Malad, Mumbai, says, "This is a kind of assembly line job that assures you a salary, but nothing more. There's not much skill or training required and people come in and go like they're working at McDonald's."

Dhaval works for an inbound call center where customers call in. He says that one cannot take a break even to go to the toilet in between calls. Cris works for an outbound call center E-serve in Malad, Mumbai, where an automatic dialer dials numbers. His work starts at 10:30 PM but there is no fixed ending time. He has to log out each time he takes a break. He has to complete six hours of log-in time, no matter how long it takes and is paid only for the log-in hours.

Many callers hang up or use foul language over the telephone. CSEs are trained to hit the mute button in order to be unheard and listen patiently without interruption. Girls sometimes get asked out over the telephone. Also the US has strict Telemarketing laws and one can be sued for calling unlisted numbers for sales.

Mayur, who works for Epicentre in Malad, Mumbai, states that he misses Indian holidays and that he has to work even on Diwali and New Year's Eve. "One has no social life and one loses touch with friends," adds Darion, a CSE at Prudential (PPMS). Sameer and Nikita, both having worked the night shift from 2:30 to 10:00 AM, complained about health problems due to lack of sleep. Sameer could not adjust his sleep cycle to sleep during the day. As a result he was always stressed. His nightmare was when he had 159 calls on hold to attend to. Nikita developed liver and eye infections.

Most of the youth working in call centers are aware that it is an interim two-year stint—wage labor rather than a career option. Reasons for joining a call center are varied. The biggest attraction is the money. Although call center employees in India are paid only 10–15 per cent of the salary of their American counterparts, it is considered adequate by Indian standards.

Outsourcing Elsewhere

With the increase in opposition against outsourcing several states in the US are planning regulations to ban government operations from being shifted abroad. Thus, this great Indian dream could soon come to an end.

Cadjetai Fernandes, economics teacher at Xavier's College says, "The employment benefits of Call centers are only for a short term and will not last for a long time. In such a scenario, thousands of graduates will be left in the lurch." Already countries like China and Philippines are gearing up to take India head-on. According to the *Outlook Magazine*, China has made English compulsory at all levels of education. Research reveals that Americans find it easier to understand Filipino English speakers than Indians.

Whether the call center industry moves elsewhere or not, the real beneficiary will always be the developed countries. While US based companies work during the day, their back offices in India and other developing countries continue their work even while they sleep. While developed countries reap the benefits, the fringe "benefits" are shared among the underdogs. The larger piece of the pie will go to the one who bids the lowest.

———■———

Some 180 million children in developing countries are in the labor force, according to The State of the World's Children 2005, *the annual report by the United Nations Children's Fund (UNICEF). Children as young as five years old work in homes, factories, and marketplaces. They work for little or no pay, and much of the work they perform is hazardous. Also, when children work, they don't go to school. As trade barriers fall, and local economies globalize, advocates for children are looking for practical solutions to this difficult problem. One idea is to encourage consumers to demand products manufactured without using child labor.*

As Suzanne Charlé of the Ford Foundation discovered, RUGMARK is a global nonprofit organization working to end illegal child labor in the carpet industry and offer education opportunities to children in India, Nepal, and Pakistan. By purchasing rugs with the RUGMARK label, consumers in the United States know that they are buying a product that was not made by children. —*AM*

From "Children of the Looms"
by Suzanne Charlé
Ford Foundation Report, Spring 2001

Kathmandu, Nepal—In the Kathmandu Valley, the packed-mud playground of the Hamro Gar school was alive with activity. The huge-eyed Buddha of Swayanbhunath temple gazed down from his mountaintop aerie as children nervously prepared to put on a play. Jhalak Man Tamang, a small boy of about 13—he doesn't know his exact age—calmly waited for his cue. He had rehearsed his lines and knew them well. As for his character, that was no problem, either: The story, about the sale of young boys into the Nepalese carpet industry and their subsequent trials, was one he knew well. Like the 14-year-old playwright and his fellow actors, Jhalak had been forced to work on carpets bound for export to the United States and Europe before he was brought to Hamro Gar—literally, "Our Home."

Jhalak, one of an estimated 1,800 children under the age of 14 illegally employed by Nepal's carpet industry, found his new home through the efforts of a program called RUGMARK, in which carpet manufacturers and exporters in India, Nepal and Pakistan join with American and European importers and nongovernmental organizations to assure that no child labor is used in creating the beautiful hand-knotted rugs. Factory owners and subcontractors agree not to employ children, and RUGMARK representatives make regular, unannounced inspections to make sure they comply. Those that do are given RUGMARK labels—each label with a number corresponding to the specific carpet made on a specific loom—assuring consumers in the United States and Europe that the carpets are child-labor free. Children found on the looms are either returned to their parents and sent to local schools or placed in RUGMARK-sponsored rehabilitation centers and schools, depending on their educational backgrounds.

"The ultimate goal is to break the cycle of poverty by moving children out of factories into schools," says Terry Collingsworth, general counsel for the International Labor Rights Fund in Washington, D.C., who spent a number of years in Nepal working on labor conditions issues.

Jhalak's story is typical: An orphan from an early age, he worked on his uncle's small farm, taking the family cow every day to the jungle. One day, a family friend came and offered to take him away from village life, saying that in Kathmandu, Jhalak could go to school while working at his home. Once in the city, the man broke his promise and sold Jhalak to a carpet master, who forced him to learn how to knot wool rugs on heavy wooden looms. Workdays started at 4 AM and went on until 11 at night; the earthen floor of the factory was Jhalak's bed. When the owner had a rush order, Jhalak and the other boys would have to work through the entire night. The owner was so strict that he even complained when Jhalak had to relieve himself. (That part wasn't in the play—Jhalak says it wouldn't have been polite.) He never saw any money. He never had a chance to play except when electricity failed.

A year ago in April, a RUGMARK inspector entered the factory—the exporter who contracted for the carpets had just joined the program. The other boys followed the loom master's orders to run and hide. But Jhalak stood his ground, and after the inspector explained the employment laws and offered him a chance to live at the RUGMARK rehabilitation center, the boy gladly accepted.

Jhalak is one of more than 1,700 children rescued from the looms in India and Nepal since 1995; more than 1,200 are studying in RUGMARK schools and rehabilitation centers.

During the same period, RUGMARK has signed up 130 Nepalese carpet exporters, who manufacture about 65 percent of the nation's rugs in 412 factories. In India, the program licenses 226 exporters, who sell rugs from 28,000 looms— over 15 percent of all those registered by the government. These exporters have shipped more than 2.1 million rugs bearing the RUGMARK label to Europe and the United States. The fees paid by licensed exporters—.25 percent of the cost of the rugs—go for inspections; importers who join the program contribute 1.75 percent, which supports schools and staff. (The India program, which was originally backed by UNESCO and the German Development Agency, is now self-sufficient; Nepal still receives funds from those agencies and the Asian-American Free Labor Institute.)

The program is an integral part of a larger public campaign to stop child labor. An editorial in *The Kathmandu Post* observed that: "Although legal remedies remain a valid and continuing concern, there is a call for more practical supplemental approaches to protect working children. . . . Nepal RUGMARK Foundation . . . is doing some commendable work. The novelty of the programme rests on its ability to work with the carpet industries through a child labour free carpet certification system, which has already helped to restore childhood to hundreds of carpet children." The writer and others point out that while the numbers of children found in some industries, such as brick making, has increased or remained constant, the number of children in Nepal's carpet industry has dropped from 11 percent of the work force to less than 2 percent.

Indian child-labor activists and members of the carpet industry in India and Germany launched the RUGMARK program in 1995. "There are laws on the books in India banning children from working in the carpet industry. The Indian Constitution prohibits work by children under 14 years old," notes Pharis Harvey, executive director of the International Labor Rights Fund and a member of the RUGMARK U.S.A. board. There are similar laws in Nepal and Pakistan. "Enforcement is a whole other thing."

India's export of hand-knotted carpets grew from $65 million in 1979 to $229 million in 1983; an estimated 100,000 children were working on almost as many looms dotted across India's "carpet belt," a 100,000-square-mile swath stretching northwest from the holy city of Varanasi in northern India. In 1985 a documentary about the child-labor situation spurred angry criticism in Europe. A consumer awareness campaign in 1990 sent demand for the hand-knotted carpets plummeting, and by 1993 India's exports had dropped to $152 million. The same year, it was estimated that 300,000 children were working on the looms in India.

In the United States, Senator Tom Harkin sponsored the Pease-Harkin bill, starting in the mid-1990's. Had it passed, it would have banned all goods produced with child labor. (In 2000 Harkin, now a board member of RUGMARK U.S.A., had more luck in pushing through an amendment to the Trade and Development Act requiring all countries receiving trade benefits under the Generalized System of Preferences to ratify and implement Convention 182, which seeks to eliminate the worst forms of child labor. U.S. customs has yet to confiscate any carpet imports, however, explaining that the burden of proof of indentured and forced child labor lies elsewhere.)

In India, a group of carpet manufacturers and exporters— nervous about the bill in the United States and a possible consumer boycott in Europe—turned to Kailish Satyarthi, leader of the South Asian Coalition on Child Servitude (SACCS), an umbrella group of NGO's working to end child labor. After a number of false starts, RUGMARK was established. The first years were difficult. In some villages, bands of loom owners physically attacked inspectors. And the number of child workers found far exceeded the available space in RUGMARK-sponsored schools. Taken off the looms, many ended up in the streets, easy prey for drug and prostitution gangs. "It was like a flood," says Rashid Raza, RUGMARK India coordinator based in Gopiganj. Today, he says, that problem has been solved, thanks to better compliance by licensees' subcontractors, the rehabilitation center in Gopiganj and four other RUGMARK schools in the carpet belt—one of which was built with funds from Nasser Rahmanan, a U.S. importer and RUGMARK board member.

In Nepal's Kathmandu Valley, the brightly colored prayer flags that ripple in the wind above simple brick buildings hint at the history and pedigree of its carpet industry, which started four decades ago when tens of thousands of Tibetans fled their homeland in 1959 after an invasion by Chinese troops. Many refugees who settled in Kathmandu had left everything behind save one talent: the age-old technique of hand-knotting rugs used for prayer and covering doors and windows. In an effort to help the Tibetans earn a living in a strange land, the Swiss Association for Technical Assistance, working with the Nepalese government, gave seed money for looms and the raw material for carpets.

"The designs in the beginning were typical Tibetan, and the small rugs were sold as artifacts in the local market," explains Saroj Rai, executive director of RUGMARK Nepal. "The first commercial export of the 'Tibetan' carpets from Nepal went to Switzerland in 1964. Soon, European carpet traders recognized the possibilities of bringing their own designs and having the carpets made in Nepal. In the 1980's, the annual growth rate was as high as 45 percent, and by early 1990, carpets became the number one export item for Nepal."

Today, there are about 1,000 carpet factories in Nepal, 800 of which export $135-million worth of hand-knotted carpets to Europe and the United States. Virtually all of the factories are located in the Kathmandu Valley, an area roughly the size of London or San Francisco. Fifty thousand work as weavers, another 100,000 are employed in carding, spinning, dying, washing, transport and other rug-related tasks. Generally, children are found on the looms because the skills are relatively easy to learn, but some are said to participate in almost every stage of carpet making.

Most of the child laborers come from the rocky recesses of the Himalayas or the crowded, fertile fields of the Terai, where poor farms cannot support the growing population. Some youngsters find their own way to the factories, lured by dreams of new clothes, two meals a day, a chance to watch TV. Most, however, are forced into the industry by adults. Some work beside parents in the factories; others are brought in by loom masters who comb the countryside looking for fresh recruits, making deals with greedy relatives, even indebted parents.

Such practices appalled Sulochana Shrasta Shah, a mathematician who started Formation Carpets after a change in university administration sidetracked her career as an academic. "When I first started, I wasn't directly aware of child labor. I remember walking around the factory, seeing the faces, sending children back home." But soon enough she understood what was going on: To fill all the seats at the looms, the loom master with whom the factory owner contracts often recruits family members. In some cases, children show up with parents who have no other resources for them during the work day. "How would people allow their children to sit on the loom?" Shrasta Shah would ask. "Then I realized: The parents simply are not in a position to bring up their children!"

Shrasta Shah opened a school and a day-care center at her factory and established strict rules—be neat in your appearance and at the loom, be on time, put your children in the school—and in the mid-1990's, along with some other socially responsible factory owners, she helped build support for RUGMARK Nepal. The response was dramatic: Faced with loss of business from Germany, factory owners representing about 65 percent of all of Nepal's exports signed up to become licensees. Shrasta Shah's importers in Germany and the United States supported her efforts.

"Manufacturers in Nepal realized they would lose all their business if they could not assure the consumer that their carpets were child-labor free," she says. RUGMARK Nepal essentially allowed the industry to offer something that competing industries in other countries could not. "It is a competitive advantage."

Aware of India's early problems, RUGMARK Nepal found NGO's with experience in education to set up two rehabilitation centers and three schools. In 2000, RUGMARK Nepal's four inspectors made some 14,000 unscheduled visits to licensees' factories and subcontractors. Riding his motorcycle, Kedar Khatiwada can make as many as 16 inspections in a day. Some factories are models of virtue; children are never found on the looms, only in factory-sponsored schools. Others are more problematic, and these are visited more often. As a back up, NGO's are asked to make random checks of licensed factories; the news media and the public are also encouraged to report any children seen on RUGMARK looms. Even the police have been known to give tip-offs.

Factory owners get the message. "No children work on the looms here," says the owner of a 16-loom operation who recently joined at the request of a foreign client. "There are too many inspections."

The first time a child is found on a loom, the licensee is given a warning. The second time, he must appear before the RUGMARK officials at the office and discuss the situation. A third offense means that the license is pulled. So far, two have been revoked.

Compared with RUGMARK Nepal licensees—even unenthusiastic ones—unlicensed factories can be jarring. A recent visitor to one found eight looms crowded into a low-ceilinged room lit by a single bulb hanging from a frayed wire. Clouds of wool fuzz drifted in the dusty air. Though the temperature outside was just above freezing, there was no heat. A woman in her early twenties sat at a two-person loom, one child at her breast, another crawling on her lap, a third darting in and out of the dank room like a barn swallow, screaming and yelling with a brigade of children who ran barefoot through piles of debris and stagnant puddles of dye-colored water.

The woman explained that she started working on the looms when she was 10. Her parents came from the Terai district and did not have enough land to support the family. She had never gone to school but hopes to send her children—if she can manage to pull together enough money. "There are three children, and only one husband," she said simply. "If I have enough money, I want to send them to school. If not, I will put them to work."

Such deep poverty is a constant threat to the RUGMARK system, according to Narayan Bhattarai, head of licensing and inspections. Not only do parents put their children to work; some, he says, are so desperate and they find the program so attractive that they actually place the child on the loom so that he or she will be found by the inspectors and taken to the rehabilitation center.

"It's a critical balance of helping the children but not sending a counterproductive message to the community," Saroj Rai added.

To this end, RUGMARK has been focusing on community-based rehabilitation. When possible, children are returned to their families and, if necessary, given stipends for schooling, rather than moving them into the RUGMARK boarding schools. Pavita Lama, a 14-year-old girl found working on a loom by Kedar Khatiwada, is now enrolled at a local school near the single room she shares with a younger brother and her parents, both of whom work in a nearby carpet factory. When Khatiwada made a surprise visit recently, Pavita took a break from studying for exams to thank him for RUGMARK's financial support that pays for her books, school fees and uniforms. She hopes one day to become a teacher, she said, or perhaps a doctor.

———◼———

Western countries' push for free markets and democracy in poorer countries can create an explosive mix, warns Yale University law professor Amy Chua. When open markets provide wealth to a privileged minority, and new democracy suddenly empowers a struggling majority, the result can be economic turmoil and ethnic violence, especially in developing countries, she writes in her book World on Fire.

This is a personal subject for Chua, who is from an ethnic Chinese family in the Philippines. In this developing country, the small ethnic Chinese population controls much of the wealth, while 40 percent of Filipinos live in extreme poverty. The economic imbalance, coupled with ethnic differences, has fueled resentment and even violence. Chua warns of the consequences when Western countries, especially the United States, try to spread their models of democracy and capitalism too quickly in countries unprepared for rapid change. She points to a rise in anti-American feelings and acts of terrorism as possible results. —AM

From *World on Fire: How Exporting Free Market Democracy Breeds Ethnic Hatred and Global Instability*
by Amy Chua
2004

One beautiful blue morning in September 1994, I received a call from my mother in California. In a hushed voice, she told me that my Aunt Leona, my father's twin sister, had been murdered in her home in the Philippines, her throat slit by her chauffeur. My mother broke the news to me in our native Hokkien Chinese dialect. But "murder" she said in English, as if to wall off the act from the family, through language.

The murder of a relative is horrible for anyone, anywhere. My father's grief was impenetrable; to this day, he has not broken his silence on the subject. For the rest of the family, though, there was an added element of disgrace. For the Chinese, luck is a moral attribute, and a lucky person would never be murdered. Like having a birth defect, or marrying a Filipino, being murdered is shameful.

My three younger sisters and I were very fond of my Aunt Leona, who was petite and quirky and had never married. Like many wealthy Filipino Chinese, she had all kinds of bank accounts in Honolulu, San Francisco, and Chicago. She visited us in the United States regularly. She and my father—Leona and Leon—were close, as only twins can be. Having no children of her own, she doted on her nieces and showered us with trinkets. As we grew older the trinkets became treasures. On my tenth birthday she gave me ten small diamonds, wrapped up in toilet paper. My aunt loved diamonds and bought them up by the dozen, concealing them in empty Elizabeth Arden face moisturizer jars, some right on her bathroom shelf. She liked accumulating things. When we ate at McDonald's, she stuffed her Gucci purse with free ketchups.

According to the police report, my Aunt Leona, "a 58-year-old single woman," was killed in her living room with "a butcher's knife" at approximately 8:00 PM on September 12, 1994. Two of her maids were questioned and confessed that Nilo Abique, my aunt's chauffeur, had planned and executed the murder with their knowledge and assistance. "A few hours before the actual killing, respondent was seen sharpening the knife allegedly used in the crime." After the killing, "respondent joined the two witnesses and told them that their employer was dead. At the time, he was wearing a pair of bloodied white gloves and was still holding a knife, also with traces of blood." But Abique, the report went on to say, had "disappeared," with the warrant for his arrest outstanding. The two maids were released.

Meanwhile, my relatives arranged a private funeral for my aunt, in the prestigious Chinese cemetery in Manila where many of my ancestors are buried in a great, white marble tomb. According to the feng shui monks who were consulted, because of the violent nature of her death, my aunt could not be buried with the rest of the family, else more bad luck would strike her surviving kin. So she was placed in her own smaller vault, next to—but not touching—the main family tomb.

After the funeral, I asked one of my uncles whether there had been any further developments in the murder investigation. He replied tersely that the killer had not been found. His wife explained that the Manila police had essentially closed the case.

I could not understand my relatives' matter-of-fact, almost indifferent attitude. Why were they not more shocked that my aunt had been killed in cold blood, by people who worked for her, lived with her, saw her every day? Why were they not outraged that the maids had been released? When I pressed my uncle, he was short with me. "That's the way things are here," he said. "This is the Philippines—not America."

My uncle was not simply being callous. As it turns out, my aunt's death is part of a common pattern. Hundreds of Chinese in the Philippines are kidnapped every year, almost invariably by ethnic Filipinos. Many victims, often children, are brutally murdered, even after ransom is paid. Other Chinese, like my aunt, are killed without a kidnapping, usually in connection with a robbery. Nor is it unusual that my aunt's killer was never apprehended. The policeman in the Philippines, all poor ethnic Filipinos themselves, are notoriously unmotivated in these cases. When asked by a Western journalist why it is so frequently the Chinese who are targeted, one grinning Filipino policeman explained that it was because "they have more money."[1]

My family is part of the Philippines' tiny but entrepreneurial, economically powerful Chinese minority. Just one percent of the population, Chinese Filipinos control as much as 60 percent of the private economy, including the country's four major airlines and almost all of the country's banks, hotels, shopping malls, and major conglomerates.[2] My own family in Manila runs a plastics conglomerate. Unlike taipans Lucio Tan, Henry Sy, or John Gokongwei, my relatives are only "third-tier" Chinese tycoons. Still, they own swaths of prime real estate and several vacation homes. They also have safe deposit boxes full of gold bars, each one roughly the size of a Snickers bar, but strangely heavy. I myself have such a bar:

My Aunt Leona Federal Expressed it to me as a law school graduation present a few years before she died.

Since my aunt's murder, one childhood memory keeps haunting me. I was eight, staying at my family's splendid hacienda-style house in Manila. It was before dawn, still dark. Wide awake, I decided to get a drink from the kitchen. I must have gone down an extra flight of stairs, because I literally stumbled onto six male bodies.

I had found the male servants' quarters. My family's house-boys, gardeners, and chauffeurs—I sometimes imagine that Nilo Abique was among those men—were sleeping on mats on a dirt floor. The place stank of sweat and urine. I was horrified.

Later that day I mentioned the incident to my Aunt Leona, who laughed affectionately and explained that the servants—there were perhaps twenty living on the premises, all ethnic Filipinos—were fortunate to be working for our family. If not for their positions, they would be living among rats and open sewers without even a roof over their heads.

A Filipino maid then walked in; I remember that she had a bowl of food for my aunt's Pekingese. My aunt took the bowl but kept talking as if the maid were not there. The Filipinos, she continued—in Chinese, but plainly not caring whether the maid understood or not—were lazy and unintelligent and didn't really want to do much else. If they didn't like working for us, they were free to leave at any time. After all, my aunt said, they were employees, not slaves.

Nearly two-thirds of the roughly 80 million ethnic Filipinos in the Philippines live on less than two dollars a day. Forty percent of all rural Filipinos own no land. Almost a third have no access to sanitation.[3]

But that's not the worst of it. Poverty alone never is. Poverty by itself does not make people kill. To poverty must be added indignity, hopelessness, and grievance.

In the Philippines, millions of Filipinos work for Chinese; almost no Chinese work for Filipinos. The Chinese dominate industry and commerce at every level of society. Global markets intensify this dominance: When foreign investors do business in the Philippines, they deal almost exclusively with Chinese. Apart from a handful of corrupt politicians and a few aristocratic Spanish mestizo families, all of the Philippines' billionaires are of Chinese descent. By contrast, all menial jobs in the Philippines are filled by Filipinos. All peasants are Filipinos. All domestic servants and squatters are Filipinos. In Manila, thousands of ethnic Filipinos used to live on or around the Payatas garbage dump: a twelve-block-wide mountain of fermenting refuse known as the Promised Land. By scavenging through rotting food and dead animal carcasses, the squatters were able to eke out a living. In July 2000, as a result of accumulating methane gas, the garbage mountain imploded and collapsed, smothering over a hundred people, including many young children.

When I asked an uncle about the Payatas explosion, he responded with annoyance. "Why does everyone want to talk about that? It's the worst thing for foreign investment." I wasn't surprised. My relatives live literally walled off from the Filipino masses, in a posh, all-Chinese residential enclave, on streets named Harvard, Yale, Stanford, and Princeton. The entry points are guarded by armed, private security forces.

Each time I think of Nilo Abique—he was six-foot-two and my aunt was four-feet-eleven-inches tall—I find myself welling up with a hatred and revulsion so intense it is actually consoling. But over time I have also had glimpses of how the Chinese must look to the vast majority of Filipinos, to someone like Abique: as exploiters, as foreign intruders, their wealth inexplicable, their superiority intolerable. I will never forget the entry in the police report for Abique's "motive for murder." The motive given was not robbery, despite the jewels and money the chauffeur was said to have taken. Instead, for motive, there was just one word—"Revenge."

My aunt's killing was just a pinprick in a world more violent than most of us ever imagined. In America we read about acts of mass slaughter and savagery; at first in faraway places, now coming closer and closer to home. We do not understand what connects these acts. Nor do we understand the role we have played in bringing them about.

In the Serbian concentration camps of the early 1990s, the women prisoners were raped over and over, many times a day, often with broken bottles, often together with their daughters. The men, if they were lucky, were beaten to death as their Serbian guards sang national anthems; if they were not so fortunate, they were castrated or, at gunpoint, forced to castrate their fellow prisoners, sometimes with their own teeth. In all, thousands were tortured and executed.[4]

In Rwanda in 1994, ordinary Hutus killed eight hundred thousand Tutsis over a period of three months, typically hacking them to death with machetes. Young children would come home to find their mothers, fathers, sisters, and brothers on the living room floor, in piles of severed heads and limbs.[5]

In Jakarta in 1998, screaming Indonesian mobs torched, smashed, and looted hundreds of Chinese shops and homes, leaving over two thousand dead. One who survived—a fourteen-year-old Chinese girl—later committed suicide by taking rat poison. She had been gang-raped and genitally mutilated in front of her parents.[6]

In Israel in 1998, a suicide bomber driving a car packed with explosives rammed into a school bus filled with thirty-four Jewish children between the ages of six and eight. Over the next few years such incidents intensified, becoming daily occurrences and a powerful collective expression of Palestinian hatred. "We hate you," a senior Arafat official elaborated in April 2002. "The air hates you, the land hates you, the trees hate you, there is no purpose in your staying on this land."[7]

On September 11, 2001, Middle Eastern terrorists hijacked four American airplanes. They destroyed the World Trade Center and the southwest side of the Pentagon, crushing or incinerating approximately three thousand people. "Americans, think! Why are you hated all over the world," proclaimed a banner held by Arab demonstrators.[8]

Apart from that violence, what is the connection between these episodes? The answer lies in the relationship—increasingly, the explosive collision—between the three most powerful forces operating in the world today: markets, democracy, and ethnic hatred.

This book is about a phenomenon—pervasive outside the West yet rarely acknowledged, indeed often viewed as taboo—that turns free market democracy into an engine of ethnic conflagration. The phenomenon I refer to is that of *market-dominant minorities*: ethnic minorities who, for widely varying reasons, tend under market conditions to dominate economically, often to a startling extent, the "indigenous" majorities around them.

Market-dominant minorities can be found in every corner of the world. The Chinese are a market-dominant minority not just in the Philippines but throughout Southeast Asia. In 1998, Chinese Indonesians, only 3 percent of the population, controlled roughly 70 percent of Indonesia's private economy, including the country's largest conglomerates. More recently, in Burma, entrepreneurial Chinese have literally taken over the economies of Mandalay and Rangoon. Whites are a market-dominant minority in South Africa—and, in a more complicated sense, in Brazil, Ecuador, Guatemala, and much of Latin America. Lebanese are a market-dominant minority in West Africa. Ibo are a market-dominant minority in Nigeria. Croats were a market-dominant minority in the former Yugoslavia. And Jews are almost certainly a market-dominant minority in post-Communist Russia.

Market-dominant minorities are the Achilles' heel of free market democracy. In societies with a market-dominant ethnic minority, markets and democracy favor not just different people, or different classes, but different ethnic groups. Markets concentrate wealth, often spectacular wealth, in the hands of the market-dominant minority, while democracy increases the political power of the impoverished majority. In these circumstances the pursuit of free market democracy becomes an engine of potentially catastrophic ethnonationalism, pitting a frustrated "indigenous" majority, easily aroused by opportunistic vote-seeking politicians, against a resented, wealthy ethnic minority. This confrontation is playing out in country after country today, from Indonesia to Sierra Leone, from Zimbabwe to Venezuela, from Russia to the Middle East.

Since September 11, 2001, this confrontation has also been playing out in the United States. Americans are not an ethnic minority (although we are a national-origin minority, a close cousin). Nor is there democracy at the global level. Nevertheless, Americans today are everywhere perceived as the world's market-dominant minority, wielding outrageously disproportionate economic power relative to our size and numbers. As a result, we have become the object of mass, popular resentment and hatred of the same kind that is directed at so many other market-dominant minorities around the world.

Global anti-Americanism has many causes. One of them, ironically, is the global spread of free markets and democracy. Throughout the world, global markets are bitterly perceived as reinforcing American wealth and dominance. At the same time, global populist and democratic movements give strength, legitimacy, and voice to the impoverished, frustrated, excluded masses of the world—precisely the people, in other words, most susceptible to anti-American demagoguery. In more non-Western countries that Americans would care to admit, free and fair elections would bring to power anti-market, anti-American leaders. For the last twenty years Americans have been grandly promoting both marketization and democratization throughout the world. In the process we have directed at ourselves the anger of the damned.[9]

End Notes

1. My discussion of the kidnapping industry in the Philippines is based principally on a series of interviews I conducted in Manila during May 2001. Because law enforcement officials in the Philippines are generally thought to have close ties to kidnapping gangs, many families of kidnapped Chinese victims simply pay the demanded ransom rather than report the crime to authorities. As a result, there is little rigorous documentation of the phenomenon. For journalist accounts, see

Caroline S. Hau, "Too Much, Too Little," *Philippine Daily Inquirer*, June 15, 2001, p. 9; Abigail L. Ho, "Chinese Traders Won't Flee, Won't Invest Either," *Philippine Daily Inquirer*, August 6, 2001, p. 1; and Reginald Chua, "Country Held Hostage," *Straits Times*, February 28, 1993, p. 7.

2. Estimates of Chinese economic control in the Philippines vary somewhat, but usually hover between 50 percent and 65 percent. For an up-to-date, if slightly gossipy, report on the wealth and holdings of Chinese Filipino tycoons, see Wilson Lee Flores, "The Top Billionaires in the Philippines," *Philippine Star*, May 16, 2001. See also "A Survey of Asian Business," *The Economist*, April 7, 2001; Cecil Morella, "Ethnic Chinese Stay Ready, Hope to Ride Out Crime Wave," Agence France-Presse, April 30, 1996; and Rigoberto Tiglao, "Gung-ho in Manila," *Far Eastern Economic Review*, February 15, 1990, pp. 68–72.

3. The statistics I cite relating to poverty, health, and sanitation in the Philippines are from: "Annual Poverty Indicators Survey," released September 15, 2000, by the Income and Employment Statistics Division, National Statistics Office, Republic of Philippines; The World Bank, *World Development Report, 2000/2001* (New York: Oxford University Press, 2001); The World Bank, *Entering the Twenty-First Century: World Development Report 1999/2000* (New York: Oxford University Press, 2000); United Nations Children's Fund, UNICEF Statistical Data: The Philippines (from UNICEF website, updated December 26, 2000); and Mamerto Canlas, Mariano Miranda, Jr., and James Putzel, *Land, Poverty and Politics in the Philippines* (London: Catholic Institute for International Relations, 1988), pp. 52–53.

4. Roy Gutman, "Death Camp Horrors," *Newsday*, October 18, 1992, p. 3, and Laura Pitter, "Beaten and scarred for life in the Serbian 'rape camps,'" *South China Morning Post*, December 27, 1992, p. 8.

5. Bill Berkeley, *The Graves Are Not Yet Full*, (New York: Basic Books, 2001), p. 2.

6. See Margot Cohen, "Turning Point: Indonesia's Chinese Face a Hard Choice," *Far Eastern Economic Review*, July 30, 1998, p. 12.

7. Lee Hockstader, "Massive Attack Targets Another Palestinian City," *Washington Post*, April 4, 2002, p. A1.

8. Indira A. R. Lakshmanan, "Pakistan Backs Us, Despite Warning by Afghanistan," *Boston Globe*, September 16, 2001, p. A5.

9. I borrow this phrase from Orhan Pamuk, "The Anger of the Damned," *The New York Review of Books*, November 15, 2001.

Apparel and textile manufacturing jobs in the United States have been hit hard by new trade agreements and the elimination of tariffs and import restrictions. Today, it is much more profitable for companies to move production overseas and to import finished goods from Mexico or China. Nearly 880,000 American jobs were lost from 1993 to 2005, and thousands more are expected to be lost by 2012, according to the U.S. Bureau of Labor Statistics. In textile states such as North Carolina, widespread factory closings and layoffs have created economic instability and uncertain futures for many families. The jobs are not likely to return any time soon. In 2005, all textile and apparel quotas were eliminated for members of the World Trade Organization, opening the gates for China, the predominant textile and apparel exporter, to flood the market. Back in 2003, New York Times *reporter Ralph Blumenthal interviewed workers at a factory in San Antonio, Texas, where the last pair of Levi jeans made in America was about to roll off the assembly lines. —AM*

"Levi's Last US Workers Mourn Loss of Good Jobs"
by Ralph Blumenthal
New York Times, October 19, 2003

Clara Flores once thought she had the job of a lifetime, even, perhaps, the most solid job in America. She made blue jeans. Not just any blue jeans. Levi's. "It was the original," Flores said. "Wherever you went, it was the same Levi's blue jeans."

The $4.2 billion company was founded 150 years ago by Levi Strauss, a Bavarian immigrant who settled in San

Francisco to outfit the gold miners. It has turned out more than 3.5 billion pairs of the sturdy denim jeans with their trademark rivets at the seams and little red pocket tab, becoming an American icon.

But by the end of the year, the last pair of Levi's made in America will roll off the sewing and finishing lines at the factory in San Antonio, another casualty of the shrinking homegrown apparel industry that since 1995 has halved its domestic work force in favor of cheaper foreign labor. It will be a setback, too, for San Antonio, home to the Alamo. The city draws a throng of tourists but suffers from a string of factory closings, although Toyota is building an $800 million plant to open in 2006.

Levi Strauss & Co.'s last three Canadian plants will close in March, the company said last month. That's part of a restructuring that will cut the company's payroll to 9,750 by next year—the peak was 37,000 in 1996—and leave none of its jeans production in North America. The work will be contracted to suppliers in 50 countries, from the Caribbean to Latin America and Asia. Competitors, with few exceptions, have shifted their manufacturing to those regions or made jeans there all along.

Philip A. Marineau, who left PepsiCo in 1999 to lead family-owned Levi Strauss Co. as president and chief executive, said he saw little symbolism in the company's shutdown of production in the United States. "Consumers are used to buying products from all over the world," Marineau said from company headquarters in San Francisco. "The issue is not where they're made. For most people, that's not gut-wrenching anymore."

But it is for employees such as Flores, 54, an $18-an-hour hem sewer and president of the local of the apparel workers' union, Unite. Flores, who has worked for the company for 24 years, will soon join 819 fellow employees in San Antonio in lining up for severance benefits and possibly retraining classes and grants to start their own businesses.

Workers said the company had a progressive record on providing for its laid-off employees. But Flores noted the workers' four weeks of annual paid vacation and their family medical and dental benefits that cost them only $24 a week. She asked: "Where are we ever going to find something like this?"

CHAPTER FIVE

GLOBAL CONNECTIONS: THE FUTURE OF GLOBALIZATION

Watching as Kentucky Fried Chicken sells its dinners from Mexico to South Korea, critics of globalization raise legitimate concerns about the "Americanization" of the world. They point to American products, television shows, music, and attitudes flooding the globe, virtually drowning the world's diverse traditions. According to critics, this reduction or elimination of ethnic diversity has the potential to lower standards around the world, equating to a "dumbing down" of culture.

George Mason University economics professor Tyler Cowen takes a look at this phenomenon, but in a different light. Cowen sees that there are positive aspects to the exchange of culture and values spurred by free trade and open markets. Even while people inevitably give up some of their habits and traditions, they benefit from the creative energy sparked by cultural exchanges. With the help of the Internet and other new technology, Cowen contends, people's lives can be enriched by the interplay of art, ideas, attitudes, and even folklore from other parts of the world. Still, he acknowledges that there will be losses, such as small isolated populations with distinct languages that may vanish as the world becomes more integrated. —AM

"The Fate of Culture"
by Tyler Cowen
Wilson Quarterly, Autumn 2002

On one thing the whole world seems to agree: Globalization is
homogenizing cultures. At least a lot of countries are acting
as if that's the case. In the name of containing what the great
Canadian novelist Margaret Atwood calls "the Great Star-
Spangling Them," the Canadian government subsidizes the
nation's film industry and requires radio stations to devote a
percentage of their airtime to home-grown music, carving out
extra airplay for stars such as Celine Dion and Barenaked
Ladies. Ottawa also discouraged Borders, the American book
superstore, from entering the Canadian market out of fear that
it would not carry enough Canadian literature. The French
government spends some $3 billion annually on culture and
employs 12,000 cultural bureaucrats in an effort to preserve
its vision of a uniquely French culture. Spain, South Korea,
and Brazil place binding domestic-content requirements on
their cinemas; France and Spain do the same for television.
Until recently, India banned the sale of Coca-Cola.

The argument that markets destroy culture and diversity
comes from people across the political spectrum. Liberal political
scientist Benjamin Barber claims that the world is poised
between Jihad, a "bloody politics of identity," and McWorld, "a
bloodless economics of profit," represented by the spread of
McDonald's and American popular culture. In *False Dawn: The
Delusions of Global Capitalism* (1998), the English conservative
John Gray denounces globalization as a dangerous delusion, a
product of the hopelessly utopian Enlightenment dream of "a

single worldwide civilization in which the varied traditions and cultures of the past were superseded by a new, universal community founded in reason." Duke University's Fredric Jameson sums up the common view: "The standardization of world culture, with local popular or traditional forms driven out or dumbed down to make way for American television, American music, food, clothes, and films, has been seen by many as the very heart of globalization."

Does this growing global trade in films, music, literature, and other cultural products destroy cultural and artistic diversity or actually encourage it? Does it promise a nightmarishly homogenized McWorld or a future of artistic innovation? What will happen to cultural creativity as freedom of economic choice extends across the globe?

Critics of globalization rally around the banner of "cultural diversity," but much of the contemporary skepticism about the value of cross-cultural exchange has very little to do with diversity. Many critics simply dislike particular trends and use "diversity" as a code word for another agenda, which is often merely anti-commercial or anti-American in nature. In reality, the global exchange of cultural products is increasing diversity in ways that are seldom appreciated.

The critics tend to focus on globalization's effects on diversity across societies. Gauging diversity then becomes a matter of whether each society offers the same cultural menu, and whether societies are becoming more alike. But the concept of cultural diversity has multiple and sometimes divergent meanings. It can also refer to the variety of choices within a particular society. By that standard, globalization has brought one of the most significant increases in freedom and diversity in human history: It has liberated individuals from the tyranny of place. Growing up on an isolated farm or in a remote village, whether in the Canadian Rockies or Bangladesh, is less a limit than ever before on an individual's access to the world's cultural treasures and opportunities. No longer are one's choices completely defined by local culture. There is more cultural diversity among Canadians and Bangladeshis than ever before.

These two kinds of diversity—the *across* variety and the *within* variety—often move in opposite directions. When one society trades a new artwork to another, diversity *within* the receiving society increases (because individuals have greater choice), but diversity *across* the two societies diminishes (the two societies become more alike). The issue is not so much whether there is more or less diversity but rather *what kind* of diversity globalization brings.

In the McWorld view of things, differentiation should be visible to the naked eye—a change in the landscape, for example, as soon as we cross the border between the United States and Mexico. It's bad enough that we have Starbucks and MTV in Cleveland; we certainly don't want to see them in Mexico City. By comparing collectives (national cultures) and by emphasizing the dimension of geographic space, this standard begs the question of which kind of diversity matters. The United States and Mexico may look more similar than they once did, but the individuals in the two countries will have greater leeway to pursue different paths and to make their own cultural choices. Mexicans have the opportunity to drink frappucinos and contemplate pop art, while Americans can enjoy burritos and read the novels of Carlos Fuentes.

Many critics of globalization are also blind to the importance of diversity *over time*. If we value cultural diversity, then surely we ought to value diversity over time, or cultural change. Yet for many of diversity's self-appointed defenders, change is precisely the problem. They decry the passing of cultures and implicitly hope to freeze them at particular times—as if to say that Bali reached a state of perfection in, say, 1968, and should never change.

Finally, we need to distinguish objective diversity (how much diversity there is in the world) from what we might call operative diversity (how effectively we can enjoy that diversity). In some ways the world was very diverse in 1450, but not in a way that was of any benefit to the vast majority of the world's people. Without markets that promote cross-cultural contacts, the practical value of diversity is limited.

The critics are quite right, however, to point out that the creation of a global marketplace in entertainment and culture poses another kind of threat: the rise of mass culture and entertainment pitched to the least common denominator— the pop globalism of 'N Sync and Hollywood action films—a "dumbing down" of culture. But this is only part of the story. What these critics don't recognize is that cultural homogenization and increasing heterogeneity are not mutually exclusive alternatives. In fact, the growth of markets tends to cause the two processes to operate in tandem.

"To have great poets, there must be great audiences too," Walt Whitman once observed, and great audiences are precisely what large markets provide. It's true that they support the likes of *Survivor*, but they also supply hitherto unreachable patrons for such exotica as Navajo textiles and Cuban dance music. Instead of dying out, many local art forms are flourishing as never before in the new global marketplace, because they've been able to find so many new patrons. Although the mass audience may be "dumbed down," over time consumers in the new niche markets sharpen their tastes and perceptions. Why does New York City have a lively, varied theater scene while the sedate small town upstate does not? For two reasons: because New York can provide an audience large and affluent enough to sustain the playhouses, and because, through long exposure, those audiences have developed sufficient discernment and taste to patronize quirky off-off Broadway productions as well as blockbuster musicals and revivals. In similar fashion, consumers in the global marketplace come to support all manner of once-obscure art forms.

Around the world, growing numbers of niche consumers are pursuing a fantastic variety of cultural interests and passions, from Indonesians gamelan music to African cinema to the postcolonial fiction of Third World writers. The array of cultural choices available to a person in a single book or CD superstore would have been beyond the imagining of anybody living a century ago. The world has more experts who know more about a greater number of cultural phenomena than ever before. Even the most obscure corners of global culture have their partisans, who study and appreciate them with great fervor, often aided by the Internet and other new technologies.

To celebrate the largely unacknowledged cultural benefits of globalization, however, is not to deny its considerable costs. Globalized culture is another example of what the great political economist Joseph Schumpeter had in mind when he envisioned capitalist production as a gale of "creative destruction."

Cultural growth, like economic development, rarely comes as a steady advance on all fronts at once: While some sectors expand rapidly, others may wither away. In the gale of cultural globalization, some poor, relatively isolated non-Western societies lose out. What they lose is the peculiar *ethos* that animates their culture and makes it distinctive—the special feel or flavor of a culture, often rooted in religious belief or in shared suppositions about the nature and importance of beauty. An ethos is what provides a culture its self-confidence, its magic. These cultures depend for their survival on the absence of the very thing that globalization promotes: internal diversity.

An ethos can help relatively small groups achieve cultural miracles. The population of Renaissance Florence, for example, did not typically exceed 80,000. But a cultural ethos can be fragile. In an attempt to keep outside influences at bay, the Himalayan kingdom of Bhutan charges tourists $200 a day for the right to visit. It has no traffic lights and no city with more than 10,000 inhabitants, and the countryside is rife with poverty and malnutrition. So far, Bhutan has been able to maintain its distinctive forms of Buddhist art and belief. The list of cultural casualties, however, is quite long. It's difficult to argue, for example, the Polynesian culture is more vital today than it was before Europeans arrived, even though the Polynesians are now much better off in material terms. Materialism, alcohol, Western technologies, and (according to some) Christianity have all taken a toll. In Tahiti many traditional arts, such as the making of fine *tapa*, a kind of bark cloth used in clothing and textiles, have been neglected or abandoned because they proved uneconomical or lost status to Western goods.

Is such cultural loss worth the gains? There is no simple answer to this question. Because of widespread cross-cultural exchanges, the world as a whole has a broader menu of choices, but older cultures are forced to give way to newer ones. Some regions, in return for access to the world's cultural treasures and the ability to market their products abroad, will lose their distinctiveness. *Tragedy*, that overworked and often misused word, certainly has a place in describing their fate.

Yet most Third World cultures (like Western cultures) are fundamentally hybrids to begin with—synthetic products of multiple global influences, Western and otherwise. For them, creative destruction is nothing new, and it's misleading to describe their cultures as "indigenous." The metal knife proved a boon to many Third World sculpting and carving traditions, including those that produced the splendid totem poles of the pacific Northwest and Papua New Guinea. South African Ndebele art uses beads as an essential material in the adornment of aprons, clothing, and textiles, but the beads are not indigenous to Africa. They were first imported, from what is now the Czech Republic, in the early 19th century. Mirrors, coral, cotton cloth, and paper—key materials in the "traditional" African arts—were also acquired through contact with Europeans.

The art of cultural synthesis has a long and honorable history, so to describe today's Third World culture makers as synthesizers is hardly to denigrate them. It is, rather, the contrary emphasis on monoculture that's offensive in its implicit portrayal of non-Western artists as static, tradition-bound craftworkers, unable to embrace new influences. The ability to incorporate alien influences has long been recognized as one of the keys to creativity. The historian Herodotus ascribed the cultural vitality of the Greeks to their genius for synthesis. To varying degrees, Western cultures draw their philosophical heritage from the Greeks, their religions from the Middle East, their scientific base from the Chinese and Islamic worlds, and their core populations and languages from Europe. In other words, the foundations of the West (and of other civilizations throughout history) are also multicultural, resulting from the international exchange of goods, services, and ideas.

In historical terms, periods of cross-cultural exchange have been exciting, fruitful times. The years between 1800 and World War I, for example, saw an unprecedented increase in internationalization. The West adopted the steamship, the railroad, and the automobile to replace travel by sail or coach, and international trade, investment, and migration grew rapidly. The exchange of cultural ideas between Europe and the Americas promoted diversity and quality; it did not turn everything into homogenized pap.

The worst period of cultural decline in Western history coincided with a radical shrinking of trade frontiers. The so-called Dark Ages, which date roughly from the collapse of the Roman Empire in the fifth century AD to early medieval times, around 1100, saw a massive contraction of interregional trade and investment. The Roman Empire had fostered regular contact among peoples spread over a great stretch of the ancient world. After the empire fell, these contacts all but disappeared with the withering of trade and urban life. Architecture, painting, sculpture, literature, philosophy—reading itself—all went into decline. Medieval society and the Renaissance were, in large part, the consequence of a process of reglobalization. The West increased its contacts with the Chinese and Islamic worlds; trade fairs expanded; shipping lanes became more active; scientific ideas spread; and overland trade routes, many dormant since the time of the Romans, were re-established. This was the crucible in which modern Western culture was formed.

Cultural exchange rarely takes place on equal terms. Yet uneven as the playing field of the global economy may be, Third World arts have blossomed. The flowering of various folk arts—from Haitian naïve painting to Tuvan throat singing in Mongolia—during the past few decades has been driven largely by Western demand, materials, and technologies of production. The Inuit of Canada, for example, did not practice sculpture on a large scale until an outsider introduced them to soapstone carving in 1948. Since then, sculpture has flourished among the Inuit, and they have developed other arts, enjoying an artistic and commercial success that has allowed them to maintain many of their traditional ways of life.

Despite the American pop juggernaut, music around the world is healthier and more diverse today than ever before. Hardly swamped by output from the multinational conglomerates, local musicians have adapted international influences to their own ends. Most world music styles are of more recent origin than is commonly believed, even in supposedly "traditional" genres: The 20th century brought waves of musical innovation to most cultures, especially the large, open ones. The musical centers of the Third World—Cairo, Lagos, Rio de Janeiro—are heterogeneous and cosmopolitan cities that have welcomed new ideas and new technologies from abroad. Nonetheless, most domestic musical forms have no trouble commanding loyal audiences at home. In India, domestically produced music claims 96 percent of the market; in Egypt, 81 percent; and in Brazil, 73 percent. Cinema offers perhaps the clearest grounds for an indictment of globalized culture because Hollywood has had so much success exporting its products. Even so, in the past 20 years Hong Kong, India, China, Denmark, Iran, and Taiwan have all produced many notable or award-winning movies. The riches of African cinema remain undiscovered treasure for most viewers, and European cinema shows signs of commercial revitalization. One reason for the domestic success of overseas filmmakers is that movies often do not translate well from culture to culture: Action, adventure, and heroism are universal languages that Hollywood speaks with great skill, but comedy, drama, and other genres usually require local accents and reflections.

For similar reasons, American books do not dominate fiction bestseller lists abroad. Even the Netherlands, with fewer than 10 million people, produces most of its own bestsellers. Yet globalization often provides local writers with an international stage, and the new era has given us notable writers who practice synthesis by wedding Western literary forms to their local traditions and concerns: Salman Rushdie of India, Gabriel García Márquez of Colombia, Naquib Mahfouz of Egypt, Pramoedya Toer of Indonesia, and many others. It's not surprising that Third World writers have been among the strongest proponents of a cosmopolitan multiculturalism. Rushdie describes his work as celebrating hybridity, impurity, and mongrelization. Ghana-born Kwame Anthony Appiah believes that cosmopolitanism complements rather than destroys "rootedness," and that new and innovative forms are maintaining the diversity of world culture.

It's impossible to deny that globalization will bring the demise of some precious and irreplaceable small cultures, and for that reason we should hope that the new global cosmopolitanism does not enjoy total triumph—that places such as Bhutan will succeed not just in preserving their cultures but in sustaining cultures that continue to live and breathe.

Yet one could not hope for a world in which we all inhabited a Bhutan, or in which Bhutan was preserved merely for our own edification and amusement. One could not hope, in other words, for a world in which we lacked the chance to experience the world's diversity, or in which another people were kept isolated and poor simply to enhance the diversity available to us. Culture is, and always has been, a process of creative destruction. We might wish for the creativity without the destruction, but in this world we don't have that choice.

———■———

A globalized economy will lead to a more equitable world, according to Jagdish N. Bhagwati, professor of international economics at Columbia University. He believes that open markets and capitalism will help build better wages and working conditions, as well as end child labor in developing countries. "Capitalism is a system that, paradoxically, can destroy privilege and open up opportunity to many," writes Bhagwati, who has worked with the United Nations and the World Trade Organization.

In this article, he explores the roots of the antiglobalization movement. He finds that many young protesters are against capitalism, the actions of corporations, and the process of globalization. They want more attention given to social justice issues. In response to these critics, Bhagwati asserts that a global economy, properly managed, will lead to more rights for women, better living conditions, and higher wages. Saying that corporations generally do more good than harm, he also asks, "The question has to be, Can they help us to do even more good?" —AM

"Coping with Antiglobalization: A Trilogy of Discontents"
by Jagdish N. Bhagwati
Foreign Affairs, January/February 2002

Globalization—a focal point of hostile passions and some-times violent protests—has become a phenomenon doomed to unending controversy. Advocates cite its virtues and its inevitability. Opponents proclaim its supposed vices and vincibility. Central to many of the protests against it is a trilogy of discontents about the idea of capitalism, the process of globalization, and the behavior of corporations. And all three of these discontents have become interlinked in the minds of many protesters. Globalization's enemies see it as the worldwide extension of capitalism, with multinational corporations as its far-ranging B-52s.

As the twentieth century ended, capitalism seemed to have vanquished its rivals: fascism, communism, and socialism. The disappearance of alternative models of development provoked anguished reactions from the old anticapitalists of the postwar era, who ranged from socialists to revolutionaries and remained captive to a nostalgia for their vanished dreams.

But globalization has also fallen afoul of a younger group of critics. And the nostalgia of the fading generation cannot compete with the passions of these younger dissidents, who were so evident on the streets at recent world economic gatherings in Seattle, Washington, Prague, Quebec City, and Genoa, and who have made themselves heard on college campuses in movements such as the antisweatshop coalition.

Far too many of the young see capitalism as a system that cannot meaningfully address questions of social justice. Many of these youthful skeptics seem unaware that socialist planning in countries such as India, which replaced markets system-wide with quantitative allocations, worsened rather than improved unequal access. Such socialism produced queues that the well connected and the well endowed could jump, whereas markets allow a larger number of people to access their targets. Capitalism is a system that, paradoxically, can destroy privilege and open up economic opportunity to many—but this fact is lost on most of the system's vocal critics.

The Perils of Education

Many of today's young, virulent anticapitalists experienced their social awakenings on campuses, in fields other than economics. English, comparative literature, and sociology are all fertile breeding grounds for such dissent. Deconstructionism, as espoused by the French philosopher Jacques Derrida, has, with its advocacy of an "endless horizon of meanings," left the typical student of literature without anchor. Derrida's technique is to deconstruct every political ideology, including Marxism. Typically, however, it is capitalism that becomes the focus of these efforts, not Marxism. And this process often has nihilistic overtones, with the paradoxical result that many of its followers now turn to anarchy.

Within sociology, new literary theory and old Marxist thought have equal influence on many students. These students have contempt for economic defenses of capitalism, asserting that economics is about value whereas sociology is about values. Economists retort that as citizens they may choose ends, but as economists they choose the means for harnessing humanity's basest instincts through appropriate institutional design to produce public good.

The presumption made by many of its radical students— that sociology is a better guide to ethics than is economics—is also misplaced. Certainly sociology's related discipline, social anthropology—many of whose adherents now find their voice in nongovernmental organizations (NGOs), foundations, and the World Bank—traditionally leans toward preserving cultures, whereas economics is a tool for change. But if reducing poverty by using economic analysis to accelerate growth and thereby pull people up into gainful employment and dignified sustenance is not moral, and a compelling imperative, what is?

Apart from academic theory, other sources that today are propelling the young into anticapitalist attitudes can be found in new technologies: cable television and the Internet. These innovations help explain the dissonance that now exists in many of globalization's critics between empathy for the misery of a distant elsewhere, and an inadequate intellectual grasp of what can be done to ameliorate that distress. The resulting tension then takes the form of unhappiness with the capitalist system within which we live and anger at its apparent callousness.

As the philosopher David Hume observed, ordinarily our empathy for others diminishes as we go from our nuclear to our extended family, to our local community, to our state or county, to our nation, to our geographical region, and then to the world. But thanks to television and the Internet, the world now seems closer than our immediate neighbors. These technologies have brought images of far-off suffering into our homes. And when today's young people see and are anguished by poverty, civil wars, and famines in remote areas of the world, they have no way to cope with it in terms of rational, appropriate action. In 1999, for example, kids protesting the World Trade Organization's Seattle meeting dressed as turtles to denounce the organization—unaware that the WTO's judicial body had recently ruled in the turtles' favor. True, there are several serious NGOs with real knowledge and legitimate policy critiques, but they are not the ones agitating in the streets.

Demonizing Capitalism

Anticapitalism has turned into antiglobalization among left-wing students for reasons that are easy to see but difficult to accept. The notion that globalization is merely an external manifestation of the internal struggles that doom capitalism—and that globalization is also, in essence, the capitalist exploitation of weak nations—provides an explanation linking the two phenomena that resonates among the idealist young on the left. Capitalism, they argue, seeks globalization to benefit itself, and, in the process, harms others abroad.

Central to this perspective is the notion that "monopolies"—for that is how multinational corporations are often described today in antiglobalization literature—are at the heart of the problem. Such monopolies, it is argued, exploit rather than benefit people abroad. Globalization is thus seen as a rapacious force that delays the demise of capitalism at home and harms innocents living abroad. Such attitudes, of course, grossly exaggerate the strength of corporations, which, even when large, undercut one another through competition. Multinationals' political power is similarly often stifled by economic and national competition.

Yet the antiglobalists insist that multinationals must necessarily be bad, because global integration without globally shared regulations must surely make things too easy for international corporations. Multinationals seek profits by searching for the most likely locations to exploit workers and nations, the protesters argue, thereby putting intolerable pressure on their home states to abandon their own gains in social legislation, leading to a supposed "race to the bottom." But appealing as this scenario may appear to some, it does not withstand scrutiny. Much recent empirical work shows that the evidence for this supposed race to the bottom is practically nonexistent.

There are plenty of explanations for why corporations do not rush in to pollute rivers and the air even when there are no laws on the books to prevent them. Aside from economic reasons for not choosing environmentally unfriendly technology, the main check is provided by the fear of a bad reputation. In today's world of CNN, civil society, and the proliferation of democracy, multinationals and their host governments cannot afford to alienate their constituencies.

Fragile Alliances

The recent successes of the forces of antiglobalization can also be explained by the fortuitous alliance struck between young agitators, conventional lobbies such as the labor movement, new pressure groups such as the environmentalists, and human rights crusaders.

Seattle saw these groups merge and emerge as a set of coalitions. The "Teamsters and turtles" faction included unions, students, and environmentalists. Meanwhile, environmentalists teamed up with blue-collar unions into a "green and blue" alliance. "Labor standards" was supplanted by "labor rights" as a rallying cry, heralding the alliance of human rights activists and the unions. And the growth of the antisweatshop movement on university campuses was accomplished by students returning from summer internships with organized labor, who then brought their fellow students and their views into an alliance with the unions.

Although these partnerships have made the antiglobalizers more effective, however, the alliances themselves remain fragile. Thus after the September 11 attacks on the World Trade Center, the coalition between unions and students started to fragment, as campuses turned against the subsequent war and the unions came out for it. The turn toward violence by student protesters in Seattle, Quebec City, and Genoa also prompted union mis-givings: the rank and file of the labor movement are not sympathetic to such tactics. The fissures are now many, and the negative antiglobalization agenda is not sufficient glue to hold these disparate groups together if they head off on different trajectories.

Still, the antiglobalization movement will remain an irritant on many fronts unless the numerous false and damning assumptions it entails about capitalism, globalization, and corporations are effectively countered with reason and knowledge in the public arena. This has yet to be accomplished;

it is truly astonishing, for example, how widespread is the assumption that if capitalism has prospered and economic globalization has increased while some social ills have worsened, then the former phenomena must have caused the latter.

The chief task now before those who consider globalization favorably, then, is to confront the notion—implicit on many of the intellectual and other underpinnings of antiglobalization sentiment—that while globalization may be economically benign in the sense that it increases overall wealth, it is socially malign in terms of its impact on poverty, literacy, gender equality, cultural autonomy, and diversity. That globalization is often not the enemy of social progress but rather a friend is not that difficult to argue, once one starts thinking about the matter deeply and empirically. Take corporations again: Have they hurt women, as some claim? Japanese multinationals, as they spread throughout the world during the years of Japanese prosperity, took Japanese men with them. But these men also brought their wives: to New York, Paris, London, and other cities in the West, where the Japanese housewives saw for themselves how women could lead a better life.

This experience transformed many of these women into feminist agents of change. Meanwhile, as the economists Elizabeth Brainerd and Sandra Black have shown, wage differentials against women have decreased faster in industries that compete internationally, for such industries simply cannot afford to indulge their biases in favor of men. Women in poor countries also benefit when they find jobs in global industries. Some feminists complain that young girls are simply exploited by multinationals and sent back home as soon as they are ready for marriage, picking up no skills in the process. But ask these same girls about their experiences and one finds that the ability to work away from home can be liberating—as is the money they earn. Nonetheless, campus antisweatshop activists still accuse international corporations of exploiting foreign workers. But studies, such as that by Ann Harrison of Columbia University's School of Business, show that in some developing countries, multinationals pay their workers more than 10 percent above the going wage, at least in their own factories (as distinct from those of subcontractors or suppliers of components and parts, who may pay only the prevailing wage).

How Good Is Good Enough?

The common apprehensions about globalization's social impact are mistaken, then. But it is not sufficient to retreat to the argument that globalization is only helpful "by and large" or "more or less." Globalization's occasional downsides should still be addressed. Doing so requires imaginative institutional and policy innovation. For instance, the insecurity that freer trade seems to inculcate in many—even if not justified by economists' objective documentation of increased volatility of employment—needs to be accommodated through the provision of adjustment assistance. In poor countries that lack the resources to pay for such assistance themselves, such programs must be supported by World Bank aid focused on lubricating the globalization that this institution praises and promotes.

With the growth of civil society, there is also legitimate impatience with the speed at which globalization will deliver on the social agendas. Child labor, for example, will certainly diminish over time as growth occurs. In this sense, globalization is part of the solution, not the problem. But people want progress to go faster. Still, the way to improve globalization is not through trade sanctions, which remain the obsession of Congress and certain lobbies; sanctions are a remedy that threatens globalization by disrupting market access and tempting protectionists.

Of course, in cases of abuse that spark huge moral outrage, a widespread resort to trade sanctions might work. But in other cases, suasion, especially for social agendas that appeal to our moral sense, surely has a better chance of succeeding. This is particularly true now thanks to CNN and the NGOs. A good tongue-lashing from such outlets is more likely than sanctions to advance progressive social agendas. Indeed, sanctions may not be unproductive; they may even be counterproductive. In one case, the sheer threat to exports embodied in the proposed 1995 Harkin Child Labor Deterrence Act led to children being laid off from Bangladeshi textile factories. Female children then wound up with even worse employment: prostitution. Contrast this with the International Program for the Eradication of Child Labor run by the International Labor Organization. This effort eschews sanctions, working instead to reduce child labor by coordinating with local NGOs, interested aid donors, and cooperative host governments. The program ensures that children get to their schools, that schools are available for them in the first place, and that impoverished parents who lose a child's income are financially assisted when necessary.

A great upside of the use of moral suasion is that is joins the two great forces that increasingly characterize the twenty-first century: expanding globalization and growing civil society.

Partnership, rather than confrontation, can lead to shared success, and it is certainly worth the hassle.

Finally, corporations should be defended against ignorant, ideological, or strategic assaults. Corporations generally do good, not harm. Again, however, the question has to be, Can they help us to do even more good? Purists say that shareholders, not corporations, should be the ones to do the social good. But that argument makes little sense. Nonprofit corporations aid society's underprivileged. Columbia University uses its student and faculty resources to assist the poor in Harlem. Meanwhile, Microsoft and IBM similarly assist the communities in which they function. More corporations today need to do just that, each in its own way. Pluralism is of the essence here: no NGO, or government, has the wisdom or the right to lay down what corporations must do. Social good is multidimensional, and different corporations may and must define social responsibility, quite legitimately, in different ways in the global economy. A hundred flowers must be allowed to bloom, creating a rich garden of social action to lend more color to globalization's human face.

———■———

A respected voice in the debate on globalization, Columbia University professor Joseph E. Stiglitz is critical of the path it has taken. Stiglitz, winner of the 2001 Nobel Prize in Economics, resigned as chief economist at the World Bank in 1999 because he felt it had failed to help Asian countries during a major economic crisis. In his book, Globalization and Its Discontents, *Stiglitz argues that the institutions created to lift up the poorest nations have not always done*

*their job. In his opinion, the World Bank, the International
Monetary Fund, and the World Trade Organization have
not adequately used their vast resources to help the poor.
Instead, Wall Street and multinational corporations have
benefited most. For example, the World Bank often demands
structural adjustments that may not help the people in
developing countries; it may instead offer loans on condition
of trade liberalization or higher interest rates. Globalization
will work better, according to Stiglitz, if we care not just
about commercial and financial interests, but also about the
environment, equality, democracy, and fair trade. —AM*

From *Globalization and Its Discontents*
by Joseph E. Stiglitz
2003

Today, globalization is being challenged around the world.
There is a discontent with globalization, and rightfully so.
Globalization can be a force for good: the globalization of ideas
about democracy and of civil society have changed the way
people think, while global political movements have led to debt
relief and the treaty on land mines. Globalization has helped
hundreds of millions of people attain higher standards of living,
beyond what they, or most economists, thought imaginable
but a short while ago. The globalization of the economy has
benefited countries that took advantage of it by seeking new
markets for their exports and by welcoming foreign investment.
Even so, the countries that have benefited the most have been
those that took charge of their own destiny and recognized the
role government can play in development rather than relying on

the notion of a self-regulated market that would fix its own problems.

But for millions of people globalization has not worked. Many have actually been worse off, as they have seen their jobs destroyed and their lives become more insecure. They have felt increasingly powerless against forces beyond their control. They have seen their democracies undermined, their cultures eroded.

If globalization continues to be conducted in the way that it has been in the past, if we continue to fail to learn from our mistakes, globalization will not only succeed in promoting development but will continue to create poverty and instability. Without reform, the backlash that has already started will mount and discontent with globalization will grow.

This will be a tragedy for all of us, and especially for the billions who might otherwise have benefited. While those in the developing world stand to lose the most economically, there will be broader political ramifications that will affect the developed world too.

If the reforms outlined in this last chapter are taken seriously, then there is hope that a more humane process of globalization can be a powerful force for the good, with the vast majority of those living in the developing countries benefiting from it and welcoming it. If this is done, the discontent with globalization would have served us all well . . .

What is needed are policies for sustainable, equitable, and democratic growth. This is the reason for development. Development is not about helping a few people get rich or creating a handful of pointless protected industries that only benefit the country's elite; it is not about bringing in Prada and Benetton, Ralph Lauren or Louis Vuitton, for the urban rich and leaving the rural poor in their misery. Being able to buy Gucci handbags in Moscow department stores did not mean that country had become a market economy. Development is about transforming societies, improving the lives of the poor, enabling everyone to have a chance at success and access to health care and education.

This sort of development won't happen if only a few people dictate the policies a country must follow. Making sure that democratic decisions are made means ensuring that a broad range of economists, officials, and experts from developing countries are actively involved in this debate. It also means that there must be broad participation that goes well beyond the experts and politicians. Developing countries must take charge of their own futures. But we in the West cannot escape our responsibilities.

It's not easy to change how things are done. Bureaucracies, like people, fall into bad habits, and adapting to change can be painful. But the international institutions must undertake the perhaps painful changes that will enable them to play the role they *should* be playing to make globalization work, and work not just for the well off and the industrial countries, but for the poor and the developed nations.

The developed world needs to do its part to reform the international institutions that govern globalization. We set up these institutions and we need to work to fix them. If we are to address the legitimate concerns of those who have expressed a discontent with globalization, if we are able to make globalization work for the billions of people for whom it has not, if we are able to make globalization with human face succeed, then our voices must be raised. We cannot, we should not, stand idly by.

———■———

Georgia-born Jimmy Carter was the thirty-ninth president of the United States, serving from 1977 to 1981. He faced many foreign policy challenges during his presidency. Carter helped negotiate the Camp David Accord, the historic peace treaty between Egypt and Israel, in 1978. He also established full diplomatic relations with the People's Republic of China and negotiated the Strategic Arms Limitations Talks (SALT II) treaty with the Soviet Union. For the last fourteen months of his presidency, Carter grappled with the seizure of hostages at the U.S. Embassy in Iran. The fifty-two hostages were released the day he left office.

After leaving the White House, he dedicated himself to human rights and world peace. In 2002, the Norwegian Nobel Committee awarded Carter the Nobel Peace Prize "for his decades of untiring effort to find peaceful solutions to international conflicts, to advance democracy and human rights, and to promote economic and social development." —AM

Nobel Lecture, 2002
by Jimmy Carter
Nobelprize.org, December 10, 2002

Your Majesties, Members of the Norwegian Nobel Committee, Excellencies, Ladies and Gentlemen:

It is with a deep sense of gratitude that I accept this prize. I am grateful to my wife Rosalynn, to my colleagues at The Carter Center, and to many others who continue to seek an end to violence and suffering throughout the world. The scope and character of our Center's activities are perhaps unique, but in many other ways they are typical of the work being done by many hundreds of nongovernmental organizations that strive for human rights and peace.

Most Nobel laureates have carried out our work in safety, but there are others who have acted with great personal courage. None has provided more vivid reminders of the dangers of peacemaking than two of my friends, Anwar Sadat and Yitzhak Rabin, who gave their lives for the cause of peace in the Middle East.

Like these two heroes, my first chosen career was in the military, as a submarine officer. My shipmates and I realized that we had to be ready to fight if combat was forced upon us, and we were prepared to give our lives to defend our nation and its principles. At the same time, we always prayed fervently that our readiness would ensure that there would be no war.

Later, as President and as Commander-in-Chief of our armed forces, I was one of those who bore the sobering responsibility of maintaining global stability during the height of the Cold War, as the world's two superpowers confronted each other. Both sides understood that an unresolved political altercation or a serious misjudgment could lead to a nuclear holocaust. In Washington and in Moscow, we knew that we would have less than a half hour to respond after we learned that intercontinental missiles had been launched against us. There had to be a constant and delicate balancing of our great military strength with aggressive diplomacy, always seeking to build friendships with other nations, large and small, that shared a common cause.

In those days, the nuclear and conventional armaments of the United States and the Soviet Union were almost equal, but democracy ultimately prevailed because of commitments to freedom and human rights, not only by people in my country and those of our allies, but in the former Soviet empire as well. As president, I extended my public support and encouragement to Andrei Sakharov, who, although denied the right to attend the ceremony, was honored here for his personal commitments to these same ideals.

The world has changed greatly since I left the White House. Now there is only one superpower, with unprecedented military and economic strength. The coming budget for American armaments will be greater than those of the next fifteen nations combined, and there are troops from the United States in many countries throughout the world. Our gross national economy exceeds that of the three countries that follow us, and our nation's voice most often prevails as decisions are made concerning trade, humanitarian assistance, and the allocation of global wealth. This dominant status is unlikely to change in our lifetimes.

Great American power and responsibility are not unprecedented, and have been used with restraint and great benefit in the past. We have not assumed that super strength guarantees super wisdom, and we have consistently reached out to the international community to ensure that our own power and influence are tempered by the best common judgment.

Within our country, ultimate decisions are made through democratic means, which tend to moderate radical or ill-advised proposals. Constrained and inspired by historic constitutional principles, our nation has endeavored for more than two hundred years to follow the now almost universal ideals of freedom, human rights, and justice for all.

Our president, Woodrow Wilson, was honored here for promoting the League of Nations, whose two basic concepts were profoundly important: "collective security" and "self-determination." Now they are embedded in international law. Violations of these premises during the last half-century have been tragic failures, as was vividly demonstrated when the Soviet Union attempted to conquer Afghanistan and when Iraq invaded Kuwait.

After the Second World War, American Secretary of State Cordell Hull received this prize for his role in founding the United Nations. His successor, General George C. Marshall, was recognized because of his efforts to help rebuild Europe, without excluding the vanquished nations of Italy and Germany. This was a historic example of respecting human rights at the international level.

Ladies and gentlemen:

Twelve years ago, President Mikhail Gorbachev received your recognition for his preeminent role in ending the Cold War that had lasted fifty years.

But instead of entering a millennium of peace, the world is now, in many ways, a more dangerous place. The greater ease of travel and communication has not been matched by equal understanding and mutual respect. There is a plethora of civil wars, unrestrained by rules of the Geneva Convention, within which an overwhelming portion of the casualties are unarmed civilians who have no ability to defend themselves. And recent appalling acts of terrorism have reminded us that no nations, even superpowers, are invulnerable.

It is clear that global challenges must be met with an emphasis on peace, in harmony with others, with strong alliances and international consensus. Imperfect as it may be, there is no doubt that this can best be done through the United Nations, which Ralph Bunche described here in this same forum as exhibiting a "fortunate flexibility"—not merely to preserve peace but also to make change, even radical change, without violence.

He went on to say: "To suggest that war can prevent war is a base play on words and a despicable form of warmongering. The objective of any who sincerely believe in peace clearly must be to exhaust every honorable recourse in the effort to save the peace. The world has had ample evidence that war begets only conditions that beget further war."

We must remember that today there are at least eight nuclear powers on earth, and three of them are threatening to their neighbors in areas of great international tension. For powerful countries to adopt a principle of preventive war may well set an example that can have catastrophic consequences.

If we accept the premise that the United Nations is the best avenue for the maintenance of peace, then the carefully considered decisions of the United Nations Security Council must be enforced. All too often, the alternative has proven to be uncontrollable violence and expanding spheres of hostility.

For more than half a century, following the founding of the State of Israel in 1948, the Middle East conflict has been a source of worldwide tension. At Camp David in 1978 and in Oslo in 1993, Israelis, Egyptians, and Palestinians have endorsed the only reasonable prescription for peace: United Nations Resolution 242. It condemns the acquisition of territory by force, calls for withdrawal of Israel from the occupied territories, and provides for Israelis to live securely and in harmony with their neighbors. There is no other mandate whose implementation could more profoundly improve international relationships.

Perhaps of more immediate concern is the necessity for Iraq to comply fully with the unanimous decision of the Security Council that it eliminate all weapons of mass destruction and permit unimpeded access by inspectors to confirm that this commitment has been honored. The world insists that this be done.

I thought often during my years in the White House of an admonition that we received in our small school in Plains, Georgia, from a beloved teacher, Miss Julia Coleman. She often said: "We must adjust to changing times and still hold to unchanging principles."

When I was a young boy, this same teacher also introduced me to Leo Tolstoy's novel, "War and Peace." She interpreted that powerful narrative as a reminder that the simple human attributes of goodness and truth can overcome great power. She also taught us that an individual is not swept along on a tide of inevitability but can influence even the greatest human events.

These premises have been proven by the lives of many heroes, some of whose names were little known outside their own regions until they became Nobel laureates: Albert John Lutuli, Norman Borlaug, Desmond Tutu, Elie Wiesel, Aung San Suu Kyi, Jody Williams, and even Albert Schweitzer and Mother Teresa. All of these and others have proven that even without government power—and often in opposition to it—

individuals can enhance human rights and wage peace, actively and effectively.

The Nobel Prize also profoundly magnified the inspiring global influence of Martin Luther King, Jr., the greatest leader that my native state has ever produced. On a personal note, it is unlikely that my political career beyond Georgia would have been possible without the changes brought about by the civil rights movement in the American south and throughout our nation.

On the steps of our memorial to Abraham Lincoln, Dr. King said: "I have a dream that on the red hills of Georgia the sons of former slaves and the sons of former slaveowners will be able to sit down together at a table of brotherhood."

The scourge of racism has not been vanquished, either in the red hills of our state or around the world. And yet we see ever more frequent manifestations of his dream of racial healing. In a symbolic but very genuine way, at least involving two Georgians, it is coming true in Oslo today.

I am not here as a public official, but as a citizen of a troubled world who finds hope in a growing consensus that the generally accepted goals of society are peace, freedom, human rights, environmental quality, the alleviation of suffering, and the rule of law.

During the past decades, the international community, usually under the auspices of the United Nations, has struggled to negotiate global standards that can help us achieve these essential goals. They include: the abolition of land mines and chemical weapons; an end to the testing, proliferation, and further deployment of nuclear warheads; constraints on global warming; prohibition of the death penalty, at least for children;

and an international criminal court to deter and to punish war crimes and genocide. Those agreements already adopted must be fully implemented, and others should be pursued aggressively.

We must also strive to correct the injustice of economic sanctions that seek to penalize abusive leaders but all too often inflict punishment on those who are already suffering from the abuse.

The unchanging principles of life predate modern times. I worship Jesus Christ, whom we Christians consider to be the Prince of Peace. As a Jew, he taught us to cross religious boundaries, in service and in love. He repeatedly reached out and embraced Roman conquerors, other Gentiles, and even the more despised Samaritans.

Despite theological differences, all great religions share common commitments that define our ideal secular relationships. I am convinced that Christians, Muslims, Buddhists, Hindus, Jews, and others can embrace each other in a common effort to alleviate human suffering and to espouse peace.

But the present era is a challenging and disturbing time for those whose lives are shaped by religious faith based on kindness toward each other. We have been reminded that cruel and inhuman acts can be derived from distorted theological beliefs, as suicide bombers take the lives of innocent human beings, draped falsely in the cloak of God's will. With horrible brutality, neighbors have massacred neighbors in Europe, Asia, and Africa.

In order for us human beings to commit ourselves personally to the inhumanity of war, we find it necessary first to dehumanize our opponents, which is in itself a violation of the beliefs of all religions. Once we characterize our adversaries as beyond the scope of God's mercy and grace, their lives lose all value. We deny personal responsibility when we plant landmines and, days or years later, a stranger to us—often a child—is crippled or killed. From a great distance, we launch bombs or missiles with almost total impunity, and never want to know the number or identity of the victims.

At the beginning of this new millennium I was asked to discuss, here in Oslo, the greatest challenge that the world faces. Among all the possible choices, I decided that the most serious and universal problem is the growing chasm between the richest and poorest people on earth. Citizens of the ten wealthiest countries are now seventy-five times richer than those who live in the ten poorest ones, and the separation is increasing every year, not only between nations but also within them. The results of this disparity are root causes of most of the world's unresolved problems, including starvation, illiteracy, environmental degradation, violent conflict, and unnecessary illnesses that range from Guinea worm to HIV/AIDS.

Most work of the Carter Center is in remote villages in the poorest nations of Africa, and there I have witnessed the capacity of destitute people to persevere under heartbreaking conditions. I have come to admire their judgment and wisdom, their courage and faith, and their awesome accomplishments when given a chance to use their innate abilities.

But tragically, in the industrialized world there is a terrible absence of understanding or concern about those who are enduring lives of despair and hopelessness. We have not yet made the commitment to share with others an appreciable part of our excessive wealth. This is a potentially rewarding burden that we should all be willing to assume.

Ladies and gentlemen:

War may sometimes be a necessary evil. But no matter how necessary, it is always an evil, never a good. We will not learn how to live together in peace by killing each other's children.

The bond of our common humanity is stronger than the divisiveness of our fears and prejudices. God gives us the capacity for choice. We can choose to alleviate suffering. We can choose to work together for peace. We can make these changes—and we must.

Thank you.

TIMELINE

1944 — After two world wars and the Great Depression, representatives of forty-four nations meet in New Hampshire to create a strategy for the world economy. Seeds are sown for the World Bank and the International Monetary Fund (IMF). The IMF works today to balance exchange rates, provide temporary loans to countries in debt, and offer technical assistance to countries undergoing economic changes.

1945– 1991 — The Cold War slows down the progress of a global economy.

1947 — The General Agreement on Tariffs and Trade (GATT) is adopted in Geneva, Switzerland. It goes into effect in 1948, aimed at abolishing quotas and reducing tariffs to increase trade among member nations.

1947 — The World Bank makes its first loan to France to help with postwar reconstruction. Today, the bank's mission is to fight poverty and improve the lives of people in developing countries. The bank provides loans and technical assistance to help reduce poverty, create jobs, and empower people.

1948 — The World Bank makes its first development loan to Chile.

1964 — The United Nations Conference on Trade and Development is established to promote development through trade proposals. It provides technical assistance for trade and development to Third World countries.

(continued on following page)

1980 — Debt crises in Third World countries cause many defaults on loans.

1989 — Germany celebrates the fall of the Berlin Wall, marking the end of the Cold War.

1992 — A worldwide declaration to improve the environment is made at the United Nations Conference on Environment and Development (UNCED), known as the Rio Earth Summit.

1992 — The birth of the European Union increases economic and political integration among European countries. Russia becomes a full member of the Group of Eight, the most powerful nations.

1993 — Representatives of 171 countries adopt the Vienna Declaration and Programme of Action. This plan was created by the World Conference on Human Rights to strengthen human rights, improve living standards, promote economic development, and ensure justice and equality in the world.

1994 — The North American Free Trade Agreement (NAFTA) goes into effect, opening trade between the United States, Canada, and Mexico. The World Trade Organization replaces GATT and promotes free trade by lowering tariffs and establishing an international dispute system.

1995 — At the World Summit for Social Development in Copenhagen, Denmark, international leaders vow to end world poverty.

1999 — Thousands of antiglobalization protesters gather in Seattle, Washington, to shut down the World Trade Organization meeting.

July 20, 2001 — A twenty-three-year-old protester is shot dead by police and 100 others are wounded during violent antiglobalization protests at the Group of Eight meeting in Genoa, Italy.

September 11, 2001 — Commercial planes are crashed into the World Trade Center and the Pentagon. Many people predict the attack will slow down globalization, but it doesn't.

2001 — China joins the World Trade Organization.

2005 — The Central American Free Trade Agreement (CAFTA) is passed to expand NAFTA to Central American countries. WTO textile quotas end. Chinese clothing imports to the United States increase dramatically. The Kyoto Protocol goes into effect on February 16 with 141 countries agreeing to reduce greenhouse emissions to slow global warming. The United States, Australia, and Monaco do not join.

FOR MORE INFORMATION

Web Sites

Due to the changing nature of Internet links, the Rosen Publishing Group, Inc., has developed an online list of Web sites related to the subject of this book. This site is updated regularly. Please use this link to access the list:

http://www.rosenlinks.com/canf/glob

FOR FURTHER READING

Bacon, David. *The Children of NAFTA: Labor Wars on the U.S./Mexico Border*. Berkeley, CA: University of California Press, 2004.

Bales, Kevin. *Disposable People: New Slavery in the Global Economy*. Berkeley, CA: University of California Press, 2000.

Barlow, Maude, and Tony Clarke. *Blue Gold: The Fight to Stop the Corporate Theft of the World's Water*. New York, NY: W. W. Norton & Co., April 2003.

Berger, Peter L., and Samuel P. Huntington. *Many Globalizations: Cultural Diversity in the Contemporary World*. New York, NY: Oxford University Press, 2003.

Foer, Franklin. *How Soccer Explains the World: An Unlikely Theory of Globalization*. New York, NY: HarperCollins, 2004.

French, Hilary F. *Vanishing Borders: Protecting the Planet in the Age of Globalization*. New York, NY: W. W. Norton & Co., 2000.

Friedman, Thomas L. *The World Is Flat: A Brief History of the 21st Century*. New York, NY: Farrar, Straus and Giroux, 2005.

Hoekman, Bernard M., Aaditya Mattoo, and Philip English. *Development, Trade, and the WTO: A Handbook* (World Bank Trade and Development Series). Washington, D.C.: World Bank Publications, 2002.

January, Brendan. *Globalize It!* Minneapolis, MN: 21st Century Books, 2003.

Klein, Naomi. *No Logo: No Space, No Choice, No Jobs.* London, UK: Picador, 2002.

Kuklin, Susan. *Iqbal Masih and the Crusaders Against Child Slavery.* New York, NY: Henry Holt, 1998.

Springer, Jane. *Listen to Us: The World's Working Children.* Toronto, Canada: Douglas & McIntyre/Groundwood Books, 1997.

Teichmann, Iris. *Globalization in the News.* London, UK: Franklin Watts, 2002.

Torr, James D., and Berna Miller. *Developing Nations: Current Controversies.* San Diego, CA: Greenhaven Press, 2002.

Annotated Bibliography

Bhagwati, Jagdish N. "Coping with Antiglobalization: A Trilogy of Discontents." *Foreign Affairs*, January/February 2002.
Jagdish Bhagwati, a professor of international economics at Columbia University, explores the roots of the antiglobalization movement. He finds that many protesters are against capitalism, the actions of corporations, and the process of globalization. They want more attention given to social justice issues.
Reprinted by permission of FOREIGN AFFAIRS (January/February 2002). Copyright (2002) by the Council on Foreign Relations, Inc.

Blumenthal, Ralph. "Levi's Last US Workers Mourn Loss of Good Jobs." *New York Times*, October 19, 2003.
Reporter Ralph Blumenthal visited a Levi Strauss & Co., jeans factory in San Antonio, Texas, shortly before the factory closed and the jobs went to Mexico. He interviews longtime workers, who tell him that they will not be able to find replacement jobs with the same pay and benefits.
Copyright © 2003 by The New York Times Co. Reprinted with permission.

Carter, Jimmy. "Nobel Lecture, 2002." Nobelprize.org, December 10, 2002. Retrieved on January 12, 2005 (http://nobelprize.org/peace/laureates/2002/carter-lecture.html).
Former U.S. president Jimmy Carter speaks about uniting for world peace and understanding in his speech upon receiving the 2002 Nobel Peace Prize at Oslo City Hall in Norway. The prestigious Nobel Peace Prize is given annually to a person who has made significant progress in establishing a more peaceful world.

Charlé, Suzanne. "Children of the Looms." *Ford Foundation Report*, Spring 2001.

Charlé tells about a successful program to combat child labor in the rug-making industry in several countries. By offering consumers an alternative to rugs made by children, the organization RUGMARK can be successful without having to exploit kids. Charlé is co-editor of *Indonesia Under Suharto*, a book about the history of Indonesians who were imprisoned after President Suharto took control of the country in 1965.
Reprinted with permission from the Ford Foundation.

Chua, Amy. *World on Fire: How Exporting Free Market Democracy Breeds Ethnic Hatred and Global Instability*. New York, NY: Anchor Books, 2004.

In many countries, from Zimbabwe to the Philippines, large poor populations are dominated by a wealthy ethnic minority. The rapid introduction of free-market capitalism and democracy can produce an unintended consequence—ethnic resentment and hatred against the wealthy minority, claims Yale University law professor Amy Chua. She is not against globalization, but urges more caution be taken to prevent these conflicts.
From WORLD ON FIRE: HOW EXPORTING FREE MARKET DEMOCRACY BREEDS ETHNIC HATRED AND GLOBAL INSTABILITY by Amy Chua, copyright © 2003, 2004 by Amy Chua. Used by permission of Doubleday, a division of Random House, Inc.

Cowen, Tyler. "The Fate of Culture." *Wilson Quarterly*, Autumn 2002.

Economics professor Tyler Cowen explores the positive aspects of cultural globalization in a world that is growing smaller day by day. He applauds the increased under-standing people have for each other. People gain more than they lose when cultures intermingle, says Cowen, but he acknowledges that some unique ethnic histories may vanish in a globalized world.

Excerpt taken from COWEN, TYLER; CREATIVE DESTRUCTION. *Princeton University Press. Reprinted by permission of Princeton University Press.*

Engardio, Pete, Aaron Bernstein, and Manjeet Kripalani with Frederik Balfour, Brian Grow, and Jay Greene. "The New Global Job Shift." *Business Week*, February 3, 2003.

This cover story created a huge stir when it appeared in 2003. It describes the dramatic changes in the labor market as more white-collar American jobs go overseas and technology changes the business world. A globalized economy is now impacting middle-class software engineers and finance managers, the writers discovered.

Reprinted from the Feb. 3, 2003 issue of BusinessWeek *by permission. Copyright 2003 by The McGraw-Hill Companies.*

"Free Trade on Trial: Ten Years of NAFTA." *Economist*, January 3, 2004.

The controversial 1994 free-trade agreement between the United States, Mexico, and Canada continues to raise questions a decade later. Has it improved the economies of the three countries? Has it destroyed jobs or created new and better jobs? The scorecard is mixed, reports the *Economist*. Advocates of free trade still like NAFTA, while critics say life for Mexicans has not improved and American factory workers have lost work.

© 2004 The Economist Newspaper Ltd. All rights reserved. Reprinted with permission. Further reproduction prohibited. www.economist.com.

Friedman, Thomas L. *The Lexus and the Olive Tree: Understanding Globalization*. New York, NY: Farrar, Straus, and Giroux, 1999.

Clashing values are inevitable in the globalization process, writes the *New York Times* foreign affairs columnist. He describes the tension between people wanting to be part of a globalized world while desiring to keep their history, land, families, and identity intact. Friedman says a balance has to be found between progress and tradition.

Excerpt from THE LEXUS AND THE OLIVE TREE by Thomas Friedman. Copyright © 1999, 2000 by Thomas L. Friedman. Reprinted by permission of Farrar, Straus and Giroux, LLC.

Gates, Bill H. "Shaping the Internet Age." *Internet Policy Institute*, 2000. Retrieved June 26, 2005 (http://www. microsoft.com/billgates/shapingtheinternet.asp).

In this essay, Bill Gates, the chairman and chief software architect of Microsoft, describes how the Internet is transforming all aspects of our lives. "The Internet breaks down barriers, makes the world smaller, and brings people together," writes Gates. In the business world, he writes, "it shrinks time and distance" and makes it simpler for companies—both large and small— to get things done.

Reprinted with permission from the Microsoft Corporation.

Giddens, Anthony. *Runaway World: How Globalization is Reshaping Our Lives*. New York, NY: Routledge, 2000.

British sociologist Anthony Giddens, former director of the London School of Economics, writes about how globalization is changing the world and the way we live. He describes how changes in the world economy are affecting families, cultures, and nations. As the world becomes smaller, Giddens writes, people who want a more tolerant and cosmopolitan future are clashing with fundamentalists; sometimes the result is violence.

Copyright 2000. From Runaway World: How Globalization is Reshaping Our Lives and the World *by Anthony Giddens. Reproduced by permission of Routledge/Taylor & Francis Group, LLC.*

Klein, Naomi. "Don't Fence Us In." *Guardian*, October 6, 2002.
The Canadian journalist and activist Naomi Klein describes
the fences, both visible and invisible, that prevent people
from enjoying the benefits of a globalized economy. These
barriers separate people from public resources like land
and water, restrict their ability to move across borders, and
stop them from expressing dissent or contributing to the
political process. Privatization and deregulation have
contributed to this mass exclusion, she writes.

Reprinted with permission from Naomi Klein.

Kumar, Nidhi, and Nidhi Verghese. "Money for Nothing and
Calls for Free." CorpWatch.org, February 17, 2004. Retrieved
June 26, 2005 (http://corpwatch.org/article.php?id=9968).
Call centers run by multinational corporations have hired
thousands of educated young Indian workers and helped
boost local economies, but two Indian writers question
whether these jobs are beneficial in the long run. They
cite the long, tedious working hours at call centers, and
the lack of long-term stability and opportunities for
advancement. Kumar and Verghese write for Unequal
Sphere, a project of the Social Communications Media
Department at Sophia Polytechnic in Mumbai, India.

Moberg, David. "Plunder and Profit." *In These Times*,
March 4, 2004.
With the support of the World Bank and the International
Monetary Fund, developing countries have been selling
government services to private companies. In this article,
Moberg, a senior editor for *In These Times* and a fellowship
recipient of the John D. and Catherine T. MacArthur
Foundation, writes about how government officials signed

a contract with a private company to run the municipal water system in one of Bolivia's largest cities. Afterward, local water rates skyrocketed and protests ensued.
This article is reprinted with permission from In These Times magazine, 2004, and is available at www.inthesetimes.com.

Norberg, Johan. "The Noble Feat of Nike." *Spectator*, June 7, 2003.
The antisweatshop movement targeted Nike in the 1990s for paying its workers in developing countries low wages and charging high prices for its products. Swedish writer and free-trade proponent Johan Norberg looks at the other side of the story. He points out that Nike is providing much-needed work to people in underdeveloped regions of the world.
Reprinted with permission. © The Spectator.

Nye, Joseph S., Jr. "Globalization's Democratic Deficit: How to Make International Institutions More Accountable." *Foreign Policy*, July/August, 2001.
The dean of Harvard's Kennedy School of Government believes that globalization needs to be governed with more openness and democracy. He suggests ways that the World Trade Organization, national governments, and even private corporations, special interest groups, and the press can improve accountability to the public and open their doors to dissent and different voices.
Reprinted by permission of FOREIGN AFFAIRS (July/August 2001). Copyright (2001) by the Council on Foreign Relations, Inc.

Postman, David, Jack Broom, and Florangela Davila. "Police Haul Hundreds to Jail; Downtown Seattle Declared a Restricted Zone." *Seattle Times*, December 1, 1999.
Local reporters describe the scene as crowds of antiglobalization protesters descended on Seattle, Washington, to protest the World Trade Organization's meeting in 1999. The demonstrations marked the first of many large protests

around the world against international globalization
organizations.

Copyright 1999, Seattle Times Company. Used with permission.

Pottinger, Matt, Steve Stecklow, and John J. Fialka. "Invisible
Export—A Hidden Cost of China's Growth: Mercury
Migration." *Wall Street Journal*, December 20, 2004.

Wall Street Journal reporters in this article describe the
toxic emissions of a coal-burning electric power plant in
China and the global environmental effects of that country's
booming power industry.

*WALL STREET JOURNAL. EASTERN EDITION [ONLY STAFF-PRODUCED
MATERIALS MAY BE USED] by POTTINGER, MATT; STECKLOW, STEVE and
FIALKA, JOHN J. Copyright 2004 by DOW JONES & CO INC. Reproduced with
permission of DOW JONES & CO INC in the format Other Book via Copyright
Clearance Center.*

Stiglitz, Joseph E. *Globalization and Its Discontents*. New York,
NY: W. W. Norton & Co., 2003.

The economist Joseph E. Stiglitz, winner of the Nobel Prize in
Economics, looks critically at the main institutions governing
globalization. He believes the World Bank, the World Trade
Organization, and the International Monetary Fund can be
forces for good and can help the world's poor, but only if they
are more open and reexamine the way they work. Stiglitz
was chief economist for the World Bank for three years
and served as an economic adviser to President Bill Clinton.

*From GLOBALIZATION AND ITS DISCONTENTS by Joseph E. Stiglitz. Copyright
© 2002 by Joseph E. Stiglitz. Used by permission of W. W. Norton & Company, Inc.*

Wolfensohn, James D. "A Call to Global Action." *America*,
January 8, 2001.

The longtime president of the World Bank urges the
developed world to make more effort to battle hunger and
poverty among the world's poorest people. He notes that

3 billion people live on less than $2 a day, and some 110 million children still do not attend primary school. Globalization must be "an instrument of opportunity and inclusion, not of fear and insecurity," he writes.

"A Call to Global Action," by James D. Wolfensohn originally published in America, Jan. 8, 2001 and is reprinted with permission of America Press. Copyright 2001. All rights reserved. For subscription information, visit www.americamagazine.org.

INDEX

A

Albert, Michael, 34
AIDS, 88, 92, 167
American Civil Liberties Union, 35
Americanization, 134–145
anti-Americanism, 8, 66, 120, 127, 129, 136
antiglobalization, 6, 20, 29, 32, 33–34, 48, 51, 52, 145–155

B

Bhagwati, Jagdish N., 145–146
Blumenthal, Ralph, 131
Bolivia, foreign investors and, 57–62

C

Carter, Jimmy, 10
    Nobel Prize speech, 159–168
Central American Free Trade Agreement (CAFTA), 19
China
    manufacturing/industry in, 5, 7–8, 47, 131
    pollution in, 96–104
    State Environmental Protection Administration (SEPA) of, 102, 104
    trade with, 6–7, 8, 28
Chua, Amy, 8, 120
    personal account, 120–129
Citizens' Network on Essential Services (CNES), 59, 60
communications
    electronic, 16
    satellite, 15–16

technology, 5, 11, 16–17, 44, 74, 76–79, 80
telecommunications, 50–51
Comprehensive Development Framework, 90
Cowen, Tyler, 6, 134
culture exchange, 6–7, 18, 134–145

D

democracy, globalization and, 49, 52–54, 121–129
deregulation, 7, 18, 63, 66

E

environment/environmental standards
    in China, 96–104
    protection of, 6, 7, 9–10, 20, 40, 62, 95, 156
Environmental Protection Agency (EPA), 97, 98, 99, 100
European Union, 7, 13, 18

F

Friedman, Thomas L., 9, 80
    on globalization, 81–87

G

Gates, Bill, 8, 73
    on the Internet, 74–80
General Agreement on Trade and Tariffs (GATT), 7
General Agreement on Trade in Services (GATS), 62
Giddens, Anthony, 11
    on globalization, 12–18

About the Editor

Traveling on a country road outside Bombay, India, in the 1990s, Ann Malaspina saw a young girl carrying a stack of dried cow-dung cakes on her head as she walked through a field. The dried dung is sold to use as fuel, and the girl was earning money for her family. As she researched this book, Malaspina thought about what globalization might mean for girls like the one she saw—perhaps an end to child labor, better education, and more job options in the future. A former newspaper reporter, Malaspina has been writing nonfiction books for young people since 1997. She has written on children's rights, the environment, history, and world leaders.

Photo Credits

Cover: © Don Hammond/Corbis

Designer: Gene Mollica; Series Editor: Joann Jovinelly

Photo Researcher: Gene Mollica